Spelling your way to Success

Spelling
your way to
Success

REVISED EDITION

JOSEPH MERSAND

Assistant Professor of Education
Department of Teacher Preparation
York College of the City University of New York

FRANCIS GRIFFITH

Professor of Education
Hofstra University
Hempstead, New York

BARRON'S EDUCATIONAL SERIES, INC

Woodbury, New York

All inquiries should be addressed to:
Barron's Educational Series, Inc.
113 Crossways Park Drive
Woodbury, New York 11797

Library of Congress Catalog Card No. 73-16791

Paper Edition
International Standard Book No. 0-8120-0163-X

PRINTED IN THE UNITED STATES OF AMERICA

2 3 4 5 6 7 8 9 10 11   M   3 2 1 0 9 8

Table of Contents

Introduction

Interest in spelling correctly is probably as old as writing. More than 2,000 years ago, the Greek philosopher Aristotle said:

"It is possible to spell a word correctly by chance, or because someone prompts you, but you are a scholar only if you spell it correctly *because you know how.*"

Apparently the Greek schoolboy and adult had their difficulties with spelling much the same way as so many of us today.

That spelling is troublesome and difficult to many people is obvious from the many complaints that have been made about the poor spelling practices of employees in business as well as students in high school and college. In a recent survey, one hundred presidents of the largest business concerns in the United States were asked their opinions about the competence in English of high school and college graduates of the last five to ten years. Over twenty of these executives indicated that spelling needed great improvement. Here are some typical comments:

"Inability to spell simple words used in business communications, such as *receive, recommend, all right.*"

"They cannot spell common every day words."

"Spelling is a lost art that should be revived."

"Their spelling has been atrocious."

"High school graduates exhibit a noticeable deficiency in ability to spell."

These are the opinions held not only by many business executives but by many college teachers and college presidents as well. Parents who compare their own achievements as students with those of their children today are also among the severe critics of today's spellers.

Of the production of spelling books, there seems to be no end. From the famous blue-backed speller of Noah Webster in 1783 to the ever-increasing number in our own times, books on spelling have been numerous. A new book in this field can be justified if it endeavors to combine the knowledge of the experts in the field of spelling with more effective presentation and better methods for mastering this important subject. If the author by his manner of presenting the important subject of spelling, through clearly stated rules, copious exercises, and numerous examples will make you interested in improving your spelling, then you will be well along the way to becoming a better speller. Like so many other aspects of learning, we learn best what we are interested in and what we really want to learn.

Most chapters in the book have one or more exercises designed to fix in your memory and to make habitual the principles of correct spelling. It is imperative that you do these exercises carefully. Note the errors that you have made and review until you spell these troublesome words effortlessly. A few minutes a day over a period of time should suffice to achieve your objectives. The exercises are of various types, in accordance with the best methods of teaching.

Above all, you must try to use as many of the words you have been studying as soon as and as often as possible. Memorizing the rules will not be of much help unless you apply them.

Lord Chesterfield, who said so many wise things to his son in his famous letters, also considered the subject of spelling.

"Orthography is so absolutely necessary for a man of letters, or a gentleman, that one false spelling may fix ridicule upon him for the rest of his life, and I know a man of quality who never recovered the ridicule of having spelled *wholesome* without the *w*."[1]

His remark about orthography (or correct spelling) which applied to the aristocratic gentleman of his day is now pertinent to everyone who wishes to be considered an educated man.

Even one of our founding fathers, Thomas Jefferson, expressed himself on this subject to his daughter, in whose education he was so interested:

"Take care that you never spell a word wrong. Always before you write a word, consider how it is spelled, and if you do not remember, turn to a dictionary. It produces great praise to a lady to spell well."

Whether from the viewpoint of good social etiquette, success in school and college work or promotion in your chosen profession, you cannot afford to remain a poor speller. This book will help you to become a good one.

The authors wish to express their thanks to Estelle J. Mersand and Kathryn O'D. Griffith; and to David Sharp, Mrs. Margaret C. Chandler, and Miss Gladys D. Roche for their assistance in preparing and editing the manuscript.

Joseph Mersand
Francis Griffith

[1] Lord Chesterfield, *Letters to His Son*, 1750.

Why Bother

1 To Spell Correctly?

We have all made mistakes in spelling, but that is no reason for giving up the attempt to perfect our spelling until we write each word we use correctly. Who would deny that a bad speller reveals his or her mental inefficiency as surely as does the dull or ungrammatical conversationalist? We all know that our futures are often determined by the impressions we make upon important people. We may lose that job, or that raise, or that official position because of something we have said that was not good English usage. Sometimes a slip into bad English may pass unnoticed or be forgotten, with no harm to us. A mistake in spelling, however, is always there to confront the reader. And that error becomes magnified with each reading until all the merits of our letter or article are forgotten and only the misspelling remains to point a forbidding finger at us.

Graphologists are able to deduce many things about your character merely by noting the shape of the letters, the placing of the words, or the slant of the writing. But your misspelled words reveal to the trained observer even more about you; and the revelations are usually unfavorable. Thus, by misspelling certain types of words you can show yourself to be:

Hard of hearing
Suffering from weak eyesight

Inclined to too rapid reading
Careless in your speech
Lacking in exactness in thought
Deficient in the power to associate similar things
Unable or unwilling to refer to the dictionary

These are pretty serious deficiencies to reveal in your letter of application or invitation before its receiver even sees you. Do you realize the handicap you must overcome if you are ever given a personal interview on the strength of the letter?

There is absolutely no excuse for habitual bad spelling today. Spelling has been studied scientifically by specialists, who have discovered not only the cause for bad spelling, but its cure. You can become an almost perfect speller by applying the proper remedies to your own particular spelling malady. We each suffer from a certain kind of spelling disorder. Having discovered your own particular variety of the disease, you can cure yourself; and you will never suffer from a recurrence of the same indisposition.

When you can spell correctly every word you employ without thinking twice about it, then your life, as far as your writing is concerned, will be much happier. Think of all the time saved in trips to the dictionary or in pondering over this or that spelling! Consider the saving in nervous energy; for you will no longer be uncertain of yourself, and no longer be angry because you realize your weakness and feel that you will never get out of it. You can get out of it! Thousands have discovered that correct spelling can be learned as easily as adding figures or planting flowers. If you will try to discover your special weakness and take the recommended cure you will surely improve and finally recover. But first let us discover why the English language is so difficult to spell.

Why Is Spelling So Difficult?

The ancient Egyptians using hieroglyphics in their written language had a far easier time of writing than do we. They wanted to represent the *sun* and they drew a picture of the sun. For the idea of a *bird*, they drew a bird. That must have been easy, compared with our problem. English is probably the most difficult modern language to spell. Why?

PRONUNCIATION

First, it is difficult because the pronunciation of English has changed in the many years in which it has been used. The spelling has not changed. The famous case of the *ough* words shows how many different pronunciations may result from the identical spelling.

Word	Sound
thr*ough*	$\overline{oo}$;
r*ough*	uff;
c*ough*	awf;
pl*ough*	ow;
thor*ough*	$\bar{o}$;
hicc*ough*	upp.

Because the sounds of English have changed in the course of centuries we have spelling problems today.

To show to what extremes one may go in the strangeness of English spelling consider the word *potato*. Using some of the unusual combinations in English it is possible to spell this word thus:

gh, ough, pt, eigh, bt, eau.

Here is the key:

gh	as pronounced in hiccou*gh*
ough	as pronounced in th*ough*
pt	as pronounced in *pt*omaine
eigh	as pronounced in w*eigh*
bt	as pronounced in de*bt*
eau	as pronounced in b*eau*

Try to discover why *fish* can be spelled *ghoti*.

SILENT LETTERS

Many current English words have retained as silent letters some which were pronounced in Anglo-Saxon and Middle English times. Thus the K in *Knight*, the K in *Know*, and the G in *Gnaw* were all pronounced—in the earlier periods of our language. Likewise the gh in *night* and in *tight* were once pronounced. Through the centuries, these sounds disappeared, but the letters have remained.

Many words coming to us from ancient Greek have silent initial letters which were pronounced in Greek. Examples are: *p*sychiatry, *p*seudonym, *p*neumatic, and *p*tomaine.

HOMONYMS

A third reason for the difficulty of English is found in the many words similar in pronunciation, but unlike in meaning.

These words are called *homonyms*. Consider these pairs of words:

ate	eight
air	heir
bare	bear
be	bee
beat	beet
berth	birth

There are hundreds of such pairs in our language. They have brought many a person to despair.

These peculiarities of English would not sufficiently explain why misspelling is so widespread. Personal factors also enter and these must now be discussed.

Why You Misspell

We all betray our characteristics and our feelings in strange ways. You are all aware of the identification methods by the use of fingerprints. Scientists not long ago revealed that we all have our individual "breathing curves"; and that no two of us are alike in this respect. That is only the latest means of telling human beings apart. A keen observer (and that is all Sherlock Holmes really was) can learn a wealth of information by noticing little things.

Now your mistakes in spelling tell people many things about yourself. Some of these things you may not want people to know. But once the misspelled word is on paper, there is no recall. You have to suffer the consequences, be they social ostracism, failure to get that position or raise, or loss of respect from your reader.

Consider the fate of the Secretary in Arnold Bennett's delightful comedy, "The Stepmother."

> Christine: Dismiss me, madam?
> Gardner: Cora, can you be so cruel?
> Mrs. Prout: Alas, yes! She has sinned the secretarial sin
> which is beyond forgiveness. She has misspelt.
> Gardner: Impossible!

DO YOU HEAR WHAT IS SAID?

Following is a list of words that reveal the fact that their writers are either hard of hearing, or careless in their hearing. These people have not heard the word correctly the first time and ever since they have been writing what they think they heard.

They Heard	*They Should Have Heard*
completion	complexion
expecially	especially
appropiate	appropriate
audence	audience
anchoy	anchovy
gaitfull	grateful
phamplets	pamphlets
upholsed	upholstery
washtan	washstand
litature	literature

Look over your own letters and other written work carefully from now on. Do you make such mistakes? Then you must listen very carefully and not write any word until you are certain of its correct spelling. If the speaker's pronunciation is bad and you don't fully hear what he is saying, take the trouble to look the word up in the dictionary at your first opportunity.

It is obvious that the writer of the following letter did not always hear correctly:

NO TUFFS OR FEE MAILS IN THIS BIER JOINTE.

The McPherson County commissioners said they had received this letter of application for a beer license:

Dear Sir:—

Eye wood like two open a bierplaise in this cittie. Eye woant sel too know boddie lest than 21 yrs off aige and too no fee mails a tall. Eye shure wil runn a furst klass barr widknow tuffs aloud. Eye clothes at amid knight. What the liesense kost? Rite me 2 east fill stashun for a fact actshum.

P.S. Recollect know loud place, just a pieceful resort.

DO YOU PRONOUNCE CORRECTLY?

Experts can tell at a glance not only that certain writers have imperfect hearing, but also that they do not pronounce correctly. And that is a far more serious error socially than defective hearing. It is difficult to be successful socially if one omits syllables, misplaces letters, or runs syllables together like a verbal accordion player. Good pronunciation is an indispensable asset to social and professional success.

Consider the word, *ansters*.

It is obvious that the writer meant *ancestors*, but what has happened to his speech? The entire second syllable has disappeared. Another explanation may be that the writer is nervous and speaks too hurriedly.

In Victorian novels frail, willowy maidens are described who seem too weak to pronounce the letter *r*. Thus they say

> *tw*ue for *true*;
> *tw*ee for *tree*

Such baby talk (and it is only baby talk) seems appropriate only to babies.

But a person who writes *skwambled* when she means *scrambled* is indulging either in baby talk or in an old Victorian custom that has long gone out of style. Since no woman of this modern day is anxious to be called a baby-talker or a Victorian, there is only one thing to do. Watch your pronunciation! Do not write a word until you are sure that you are pronouncing it correctly.

Do you pronounce the letter in italics? Glance at these words. You may discover syllables you hardly suspected before.

LETTERS OFTEN OMITTED
BY CARELESS SPEAKERS

priv *i* lege	enviro *n* ment
aux il *i* ary	Feb *r* uary
gover *n* ment	interp *r* eted
accompan *i* ment	lab *o* ra tory
temper *a* ment	mag *a* zine
accident *a* lly	min i *a* ture
approp *r* iate	op *e* rate
bach *e* lor	partic *u* lar

HOW ARE YOUR NERVES TODAY?

Everybody has a slip of the tongue now and then. We may be terribly anxious to say something and the words rush out pell-mell, and what a mess they make of it! That agitation is revealed when you misspell certain words. You may not want the reader to think that you are easily aroused. You may be applying for a position, where calmness and restraint are prerequisites. But your spelling will give you away.

These are words spelled in a way to reveal your emotional disturbances:

compelte	for complete;
files	for flies;
appiled	for applied.

HASTY READINGS

About 10,000 books are published in America each year. If you wanted to read all of these American books you would have to read about twenty-one books a day, every single day in the year. Of course that is impossible. We can't even get around to reading one book a day. This tremendous supply of reading matter (we have not mentioned the morning and evening newspaper, and half a dozen magazines each month) has caused the formation of the habit of hasty reading. This is, to be sure, an age of speed. We are all speeded up in our locomotion, our eating, our vocations and our reading.

There is a limit to the speed with which you can read. If you go beyond that limit, words become indistinct, blurred, and meaningless. If you boast about finishing the latest novel in two hours, the chances are you misspell many words, because you have not a clear picture of them. One can rarely read more than fifty pages an hour and derive the full benefit of the reading.

Check up on yourself. You will discover that many words which you first met in print, you misspell in your personal writings because you raced over these words instead of forming a clear picture of them in your mind.

This is not to deny the value of that type of rapid reading for a specific purpose which is called *skimming*. When you are not particularly interested in getting every idea and fact from the printed page but only some statistic or date or personal name, it would be a waste of time to read every word slowly. A rapid glance at the entire page will give you the answer you are seeking. However, this is not the type of reading for ideas, beauty of style, or for a detailed explanation. These require slower reading than skimming.

FAULTY OBSERVATION

A story is told of Toscanini, the great conductor, that illustrates his phenomenal power of observation. Of course, the world knows that he conducted entirely from memory; that he committed to memory the entire score of Respighi's *Pines of*

Rome in twenty-four hours. A certain bassoon-player wanted to be excused from a rehearsal because his bassoon needed some repairing. One of the keys would not play the note.

"What note doesn't play?" asked the maestro.

"B-flat," answered the bassoon-player.

"Never mind. Stay for the rehearsal. There are no B-flats for the bassoon parts in to-night's program."

That is careful observation. Infinite pains, hours of concentration, and nerve-wracking study went into such perfect knowledge.

How many of us will take those pains? How many of us care to observe? "Genius," said some critic, "is the infinite capacity of taking pains."

The fault of poor observation is with most of us. The reason is our inertia. It means too much trouble, and we like the path of least resistance. By failing to note the correct spelling at first, we fall into the habit of misspelling many words.

Most people, when they are doubtful about the spelling of a word, write it down two or three times. The incorrect forms do not *appear* right. We have a mental picture of the correct word. When we write the correct form, something clicks within us. We *feel* we have it right.

You will notice that those who have observed carefully have formed such a vivid picture of the word that they can instantly recall it when they want.

▶ *REMEMBER!*
CAREFUL
OBSERVATION PAYS
AND PAYS WELL

How To Become
4 | *A Good Speller*

Aristotle, the great Greek philosopher, was tutor to the future king, Alexander the Great. One day they were doing a lesson in mathematics which required many calculations. Alexander, always impatient, suddenly threw aside his work and exclaimed: "Why must I go through all these little steps? Why can't I get the answer immediately? I'm the future king!"

"There is no royal road to knowledge," answered his tutor.

There is no royal road to knowledge. There is no short cut to any branch of learning, and that is especially true for spelling. We had trouble with spelling in America long before Noah Webster published his famous speller. Nobody was ever born a perfect speller. Spellers are *made*; not born. Everyone can become a good speller by following certain scientifically prepared steps. There are some who had to learn the spelling of every word they met painfully and slowly. That was a waste of nervous energy. Time and nerve-power will be conserved, and success will be assured if you will follow the steps enumerated below. This is a prescription for good spelling that has rarely failed. Why not give it a trial?

Learn and apply the rules of spelling.

Try to discover little devices of your own that will help you to remember the spelling of words that have no rules.

EXAMPLES:

Principal: means the head of a school or the main thing.

Principle: means a rule or a truth.

Much slaughter on the battlefield of a spelling has been caused by these two enemies of peace of mind and soul. And yet one simple device will remove forever the confusion caused by them.

A princip*le* is a ru*le*. Both of these end in *le*. Now you have the whole secret. If it means a ru*le*, spell it with the *le*; the other meaning must be spelled princi*pal*. You may remember it another way. If your principal is a fine fellow, he was a PAL to you. And there you have the second sure way of remembering these two spelling demons.

STATIONARY VS. STATIONERY

These two have been fighting on our literary battle-ground ever since we can remember. You think you have the correct spelling when suddenly the other one butts in and then you're lost again.

How can you be certain? Easily. Take a lett*er*; yes, a lett*er*. That's what stationery is used for, and you'll notice that lett*er* ends in ER. Now station*ery* ends in ERY.

The other word means standing still. Think of the *a* in standing and you'll remember the ARY in station*ary*.

SEPARATE

The word sep*a*rate has long been a trouble spot.

Think of the word PART. When you sep AR ate, you take things ap ART. That will tell you to be sure to spell the word with AR.

These three devices you may use. But the best of these tricks are the ones you think up yourself. When you discover a way to spell a word that has always given you trouble, you will be so overjoyed at the discovery that you will never forget the spelling. All laws of psychology teach us that we seldom forget anything we learned with pleasure. Therefore, try to be a spelling discoverer; enjoy your latest discovery and one more spelling demon will be eliminated.

Here is a good way to prevent the confusion in spelling of *their* and *there*.

here. . . . . ⎫
(w)here. . . . . ⎬place
(t) here. . . . . ⎭

The personal pronoun must, by elimination, be *their*.

▶ *REMEMBER!*

Form your own memory devices.

CONSULT THE DICTIONARY

The dictionary is probably the most valuable book in one's library. You should form the habit of consulting it the moment you are confronted with any spelling difficulty. Don't delay. When a word bothers you, and no rule or device will help, look it up while the annoyance is fresh. This is good psychology. The sooner you remove the cause of the annoyance (the doubtful word) the more certain will you be of its disappearance as an annoyance.

The dictionary is an authority that cannot be challenged. It is much more reliable than the memory of ordinary mortals. Why worry about the spelling of a word? A glance into the dictionary will answer your question. Sometimes the same word may be spelled correctly in more than one way, and the dictionary will help you on this aspect. For example, our spellings of *labor* and *favor*, and *armor* are paralleled in England by the spellings: *labour, favour* and *armour*. The British prefer the spellings—*connexion, deflexion,* and *inflexion* to the American *connection, deflection* and *inflection*.

Invariably the British spell these words with a final RE: *centre, metre, theatre*. American spellings are: *center, meter,* and *theater*.

In all these instances, and many more, a good college dictionary like the *Webster's New Collegiate Dictionary* or its counterparts from other publishers will indicate these differences. For this purpose the special section on "Orthography" in Webster's is especially useful.

▶ *REMEMBER!*

Consult the Dictionary.

MAKE YOUR OWN SPELLING LIST

Make a list of your difficult words. Try to use these as often as the opportunity presents itself. Mark Twain, who has had no superior in American humor, and whose principles of writing deserve the respect of all who would learn, said, "Use a new word correctly three times, and it's yours." Use a word that has given *you* trouble three times correctly and you should not have any difficulty. The important thing is to use it *correctly*. Misspelling a word a number of times only fixes the misspelling more firmly. There is a popular expression to the effect that

"Practice Makes Perfect." But that should really be "Practice Makes Permanent." If we always make the same mistake, no amount of practice will do anything to improve our knowledge. Remember to use it correctly the first time.

CAREFUL LISTENING

Develop the art of listening carefully. Many people whose hearing shows no organic defect are poor listeners. They do not pay attention and consequently they don't really hear what is being said. The more cultured the topic, the more alert must the listener be. These days there is much talk in the field of economics. Terms like *government, security, conservation* are heard repeatedly. Do you hear *gover n ment* or *guvment? Scurity* or *security? Consivation* or *conservation?*

It is true that sometimes the speaker himself is at fault because his enunciation is not perfect. That does not excuse the listener, however. If a word does not seem quite clear to you, you owe it to yourself to consult the dictionary as soon as you are near one. Thus you will firmly establish that word in your mind.

▶ *REMEMBER!*

Listen attentively; look up a doubtful word; let no time be wasted.

What has just been said are general instructions. Below are the steps you are to follow in learning any particular word that has given you trouble. Don't take short cuts. Follow the instructions to the letter!

▶ *METHOD FOR*
LEARNING TO SPELL
ANY HARD WORD!

1. *Look* at your word. *Pronounce* each syllable carefully.

EXAMPLE:

in de pend ent.

2. *Close* your eyes or turn away and form a picture of the word in your mind. If the letters are not clearly before you, look at the word again, until you see it with your eyes closed.

3. *Pronounce* the word and write it at the same time. If you are not sure, try to picture the word. Be certain that you write it correctly the first time.

4. *Write* the word a second time as used in a sentence.

5. The next day write the word down as someone else reads it to you.

Rules For Spelling: The Hyphen

It is possible, of course, to consult your dictionary every time you are in doubt about the spelling of a word. The knowledge of a few helpful rules, however, will make it unnecessary for you to waste precious time in consulting the dictionary on every occasion when you are in doubt. As is true of almost all rules in English grammar, there are some exceptions to the rules in spelling, too. It is, therefore, necessary to master the exceptions as well as the rules. Study the rules, do the exercises, and try using some of the words you have studied as soon as possible. Remember that your ultimate aim in spelling is to be able to spell every word you want to use without wasting any time trying to figure out the spelling or wasting precious minutes looking up in the dictionary every word of more than two syllables.

THE HYPHEN

English is a language rich in compound words. Sometimes two nouns are combined as in *secretary-treasurer* because the new term combines the functions of both. The hyphen here shows that you are talking about one man or woman. Many compound words are adjectives formed from various parts of speech. For example, to say that a *car is of low price* seems a little archaic. (We might say: *A pearl of great price*.) Hence, we write *low-priced* car.

In describing a suit which you could wear at once after you had bought it, you could write: *a garment that was already made,* or the much shorter, *ready-made* garment.

Many hyphenated words eventually become so familiar, that they are written as one word. Certain magazines like *LIFE, TIME, NEWSWEEK,* frequently write as single words those which texts and dictionaries still hyphenate.

COMPOUND ADJECTIVES

There are eight types of such hyphenated adjectives.

Noun or adjective + participle

EXAMPLES:

fire-fighting apparatus (noun + participle)
bad-looking apples (adjective + participle)
blue-eyed girl

Noun + adjective

EXAMPLES:

city-wide campaign
lily-white hands
rose-red cheeks

Compound numbers between 21-99

EXAMPLES:

twenty-fifth person
the three hundred and *seventy-fifth* bill

Number + nouns

EXAMPLES:

the *five-year* plan
thirty-cent seats
twelve *two-year* olds

Short adverbs (best, far, ill, long, much, well)
+ participle

EXAMPLES:

best-known author
far-fetched theory
ill-gotten gains
long-needed vacation
well-looking person

Adjectives of Nationality

EXAMPLES:

Franco-Prussian War
Anglo-Saxon
Anglo-Norman

Two nouns forming an adjective

EXAMPLES:

a *father-son* banquet
a *brother-sister* act
a *mother-daughter* outfit

Verb plus other elements forming an adjective

EXAMPLES:

The *would-be* actor
The *wait-and-see* plan for peace
A *hit-and-run* driver

▶ *CAUTION!*

Avoid the hyphen

1. When the adjective follows the noun:

EXAMPLES:

She was an executive well known for her honesty.
He was a man ill fitted for the job.

2. When two independent adjectives precede the noun and are not combined:

EXAMPLES:

Napoleon wore his old blue uniform. But: *Napoleon wore his sky-blue uniform* (only one adjective).
She carried the tired old dog.

3. When an adverb modifies an adjective:

EXAMPLES:

He was a highly paid executive.
This was a nicely kept room.
It was a newly born calf.

4. When a comparative or superlative form is one of the two modifiers:

EXAMPLES:

There was no kinder hearted person in the room.
A low-priced car was desired.
But: *The lowest priced car was the Rambler.*
The mild-tempered man spoke out.

5. When the compound modifier is a proper noun of two words:

EXAMPLES:

Thomas Mann was a Nobel Prize winner.
He was the South American representative in the Security Council.

6. When one word in the compound modifier has an apostrophe:

EXAMPLES:

The first year's harvest was small.
The third century's literature was most religious.
The seventh day's fast was broken.

EXERCISE 1.

Indicate at the right whether the following words are properly hyphenated. Place a *C* if correct and an *X* if wrong.

1. well-fed cattle . . . .
2. redcheeked youngster . . . .
3. tenday reducing diet . . . .
4. a three-month delay . . . .
5. the twenty-second victim . . . .
6. badly-lit interior of the hut . . . .
7. state-wide elections . . . .
8. redeyed Susan . . . .
9. a seven-day wonder . . . .
10. the kind-hearted minister . . . .
11. hornrimmed spectacles . . . .
12. the legend of the saber toothed tiger . . . .
13. This was indeed a well kept garden . . . .
14. His ill-fated story was common knowledge . . . .
15. My sister was a red-head . . . .
16. a first class performance . . . .
17. the silver plated fork . . . .
18. the sky-blue water . . . .
19. England's far-flung empire . . . .
20. the far-off hills of Dune . . . .

COMPOUND NOUNS

By using the hyphen with two or more familiar words, new words have been added to our vocabulary.

A. Use the hyphen when two normally distinct functions are united in one person or thing.

EXAMPLES:

secretary-treasurer
fighter-bomber

▶ *CAUTION !*

Do not hyphenate double terms that represent a single office:

EXAMPLES:

Major General
Secretary of Defense
General of the Army
Lieutenant Commander
General Manager
Executive Secretary

B. When two nouns form a new noun. Usually the first acts with the force of an adjective.

EXAMPLES:

trade-mark
light-year
foot-pound

C. Sometimes a noun will be combined with another part of speech to form an entirely new noun.

EXAMPLES:

passer-by   (a noun plus a word meaning direction or motion)
son-in-law
jack-in-the-box   (a noun plus a phrase)

D. A verb may be combined with some other part of speech to make a noun.

EXAMPLES:

A *know-all*
A *do-nothing*
A *cure-all*
A *know-nothing*

(in these cases the verb plus its object makes a new noun)

EXAMPLES:

A *flare-up,*	*play-off*	A *stick-up*
A *lean-to,*	*drive-in*	A *count-down*
A *go-between,*	*shake-up*	

(Here the verbs have been combined with preposi-tions to make new nouns)

COMPOUND NUMBERS
AND FRACTIONS

Use the hyphen in numbers from twenty-one to ninety-nine.

In fractions use the hyphen when the fraction is used as an adjective.

EXAMPLES:

The three and one-half pounds of butter.
Two and one-eighth quarts of milk.

▶ *CAUTION!*

Do not use the hyphen when the fraction is not a single adjective.

EXAMPLES:

The chairman asked *one third* of the group to stay.
He drank *one half* of the cup quickly.

COMPOUNDS WITH
CERTAIN PARTICLES

A. Most compounds with *self* use the hyphen.

EXAMPLES:

self-sacrifice
self-interest
self-made man

▶ *CAUTION!*

Do not hyphenate the reflexives such as *yourself*, *himself*, *herself*, or *self* in such adjectives as *selfless*, *selfsame*.

B. The prefix *re* when it means again takes the hyphen, especially if necessary to prevent confusion.

EXAMPLES:
> *re-form* the squad
> *re-enact* the crime
> *re-emerge* from retirement

▶ *NOTE!*

Note the difference between *reform* the drunkard and *re-form* the broken line of infantry.

To eliminate the hyphen in *re-enact* and *re-emerge* might lead to mispronunciation or misunderstanding.

C. With prefixes ending in the same vowel that begins the next word.

EXAMPLES:
> *co-owner*
> *pre-election*

D. When a prefix is added to a word beginning with a capital letter.

EXAMPLES:
> *mid-Atlantic*
> *anti-Russian*
> *pro-British*

E. With titles which are preceded by *vice*, *ex*, and followed by *elect*.

EXAMPLES:
> *Vice-Admiral*
> *Vice-President*
> *Senator-elect*
> *President-elect*
> *ex-Governor*

CLEARNESS

Use a hyphen to avoid confusion of meaning.
In the following sentence something is wrong.

Did you ever see a nail polish like this?

Without the hyphen the *nail* appears to be an active agent. With the hyphen the *nail-polish* becomes what it should be.

Here are a few more boners that result when the hyphen is not used:—

1. The master like pose of John. (Sounds like an Oriental valet speaking)

2. The well kept house. (This must be a very versatile well, what with its job as water-producer, and now as house-cleaner.)

If you are ever in doubt consult this list.

These words are *never* hyphenated:

airman	nevertheless
background	outline
downstairs	pastime
farewell	railroad
headline	semicolon
inasmuch	together
keyboard	warehouse
midday	yourself

These words always have a hyphen:

brother-in-law	son-in-law
daughter-in-law	aide-de-camp
father-in-law	man-of-war
mother-in-law	runner-up
sister-in-law	jack-o'-lantern

The hyphen has another use at the end of a line in a page of writing. It is inadvisable as a general principle to divide a word at the end of the line; but if it must be done, then a hyphen is placed at the end of the line, in accordance with the rules of syllabication. The following words are always written separately:

all ready	each other
all right	*en route*
some way	every way
some day	every time
some place	*ex officio*
any day	in fact
any place	in order
by and by	in spite
by the bye	*pro tempore*
by the way	no one

EXERCISE 2.

Spell the following words correctly by inserting the hyphen where it belongs. If the word is correctly spelled, write *C* in the space to the right.

1. sisterinlaw ....
2. man of war ....
3. aidedecamp ....
4. runon sentence ....
5. down-stairs ....
6. anti American activities ....
7. ex-husband ....
8. re-emerge ....
9. self-centered child ....
10. one quarter of the population ....
11. runnerup ....
12. drivein theatre ....
13. secretary-treasurer ....
14. Lieutenant General ....
15. tradein ....
16. fire-fighting engine ....
17. pro-European policy ....
18. builtin arch ....
19. The final play-off ....
20. broken-down houses ....

Rules For Spelling: Doubling Final Consonants

Do you know the difference between *riding* a horse and *ridding* the house of undesirable visitors? Do you know when people are *hoping* and when they are *hopping?* These are some examples of words with doubled consonants. There is no reason why anyone should suffer while trying to remember whether to spell a word with one or with two final consonants, for there are rules which will take care of all cases.

How many times have you been puzzled about doubling a consonant?

Does *beginning* have two *n*'s in the middle?

Does *omitted* have two *t*'s?

Why has *benefiting* one *t*, while *admitting* has two?

These and all other questions are easily answered if you will remember a few scientific rules. There are very few rules in English as sure to help you as these.

First you must recall the meaning of the word *syllable*. Look at these words:

run   *swim*   *hop*

▶ *NOTICE!*

Each of these has a vowel in the middle and a consonant at the end. These make up one syllable and such a word is called a one-syllable word.

But look at these:

con fer   *pre fer*   *trans fer*

You notice that we have at least *two* syllables in each word.

Now we can proceed to the rules.

Notice what happens to our three friends when we add *ing*.

running

swimming

hopping

The final consonant (n, m, p) has been doubled before a suffix beginning with a vowel.

We could have added the suffix *er* and we would get

ru NN er

swi MM er

ho PP er

Again the final consonant was doubled before a suffix beginning with a vowel.

Now the rule is easy.

▶ *RULE 1*

When a one-syllable word (run) ends in one vowel (u) and one consonant (n), that consonant is doubled (nn) before a suffix beginning with a vowel (er).

Now discover for yourself what would happen to the final consonants of these words.

Word	+ ER	+ ING
hit	hiTTer	hiTTing
spin	spiNNer	spiNNing
wrap	wraPPer	wraPPing
trim	triMMer	triMMing

These words are easy.

The following words have more than one syllable but they follow the same rule as the words just described. They *double* their final consonant before a suffix beginning with a vowel.

Word	+ ER	+ ING	+ Other Suffix
admit		admiTTing	admittedly
begin	begiNNer	begiNNing	
compel		compeLLing	
confer		confeRRing	
control		controLLing	controLLable
commit		commiTTing	
equip		equiPPing	
omit		omiTTing	

These cases are all covered by another simple rule.

▶ *RULE 2*

A word of more than one syllable (occur) ending in a single vowel (u) and a single consonant (r), which has the accent on the final syllable, doubles that consonant (RR) before a suffix beginning with a vowel (occu RR ing). Remember the accent must be on the last syllable.

> *occ ur'*
> *ad mit'*
> *per mit'*

Unless the final syllable has the accent, there will be no doubling of the consonant. Thus, *benefit* will not double the *t*, because the accent is on the first syllable. *Ben e fit ing.*

Study the suffixes to the following words.
Each word satisfies three conditions.

1. It is more than one syllable.
2. The last syllable has the accent.
3. The last syllable ends in *one* vowel and *one* consonant.

Word	*+ ING*	*+ ED*	*+ Other Suffix*
abet	abe TT ing	abe TT ed	abe TT or
abhor	abho RR ing	abho RR ed	abho RR ence
admit	admi TT ing	admi TT ed	admi TT ance
allot	allo TT ing	allo TT ed	allo TT ance
annul	annu LL ing	annu LL ed	annu L ment (one L because the suffix begins with a consonant)
confer	confe RR ing	confe RR ed	confe R ence (one R because the accent is not on *FER* but *CON*)
concur	concu RR ing	concu RR ed	concu RR ence
defer	defe RR ing	defe RR ed	defe R ence (only one R because accent is *not* on last syllable)
dispel	dispe LL ing	dispe LL ed	
excel	exce LL ing	exce LL ed	
infer	infe RR ing	infe RR ed	infe R ence (one R. Why?)
occur	occu RR ing	occu RR ed	occu RR ence
omit	omi TT ing	omi TT ed	
rebel	rebe LL ing	rebe LL ed	rebe LL ion
recur	recu RR ing	recu RR ed	recu RR ence

refer	refe RR ing	refe RR ed	refe R ence (one R. Why?)
regret	regre TT ing	regre TT ed	
transfer	transfe RR ing	transfe RR ed	

SPECIAL CASE

Words ending in *C* add *K* before a suffix begin-ning with *e, i,* or *y.*

EXAMPLES:

picnic	+ *ed*—picnic **K** ed	This is done to
traffic	+ *ing*—traffic **K** ing	retain the hard
panic	+ *y*—panic **K** y	C sound in the word with the suffix.

EXERCISE 1.

Below is a list of verbs of one syllable. Add ING to each of them. Some will double their final consonant. Some will not. Why? Remember Rule 1. There must be only *one* vowel and *one* consonant.

1. cramp . . . .
2. drum . . . .
3. grin . . . .
4. hit . . . .
5. look . . . .
6. nod . . . .
7. pain . . . .
8. rest . . . .
9. rig . . . .
10. scrub . . . .

Six out of the ten doubled their consonants. The remaining four did not because they had a vowel and two con-sonants (cr a m p) or two vowels and consonant (l oo k).

Now for a few pairs of words with different meanings, depending upon the doubling of the consonants.

bar	He *barred* the door.
bare	He *bared* his arm.
din	The teacher *dinned* it into John's ear.
dine	We *dined* at four.
pin	Mary *pinned* her dress.
pine	Mary *pined* away.
plan	They *planned* a happy life.
plane	The carpenter *planed* the wood.
scrap	The two dogs *scrapped*.
scraped	Walter *scraped* his new knife on the cement floor.
wag	He *wagged* his head solemnly.
wage	He *waged* a bitter war.

Notice how the meaning is determined by the single or double consonant and why correct spelling is so important to convey your meaning. Notice these few exceptions to the rule:

chagrined, gaseous, transferable, transference, transferee, facility.

EXERCISE 2.

Write correctly the words formed as the exercise
indicates:

1. defer + ed   deferred . . . .
2. refer + ence   . . . .
3. shop + ing   . . . .
4. disapprove + al   . . . .
5. nine + teen   . . . .
6. hit + ing   . . . .
7. singe + ing   . . . .

8. lame + ous . . . .
9. control + ing . . . .
10. repel + ent . . . .
11. desir + ing . . . .
12. tire + less . . . .
13. true + ly . . . .
14. swim + er . . . .
15. trim + er . . . .
16. occur + ence . . . .
17. move + able . . . .
18. commit + ed . . . .
19. equip + age . . . .
20. excel + ing . . . .

EXERCISE 3.

Write the present participle (ing) and past participle (ed) of the following verbs. Some will double the final consonant; others will not. When in doubt, refer to the rules on doubling final consonants.

	Word	Present Participle	Past Participle
EXAMPLE:	admit	admitting	admitted
1.	adapt	. . . .	. . . .
2.	cramp	. . . .	. . . .
3.	design	. . . .	. . . .
4.	conceal	. . . .	. . . .
5.	congeal	. . . .	. . . .
6.	blot	. . . .	. . . .
7.	stop	. . . .	. . . .
8.	crush	. . . .	. . . .
9.	excel	. . . .	. . . .
10.	defer	. . . .	. . . .

11. envelop	....	....
12. extol	....	....
13. flutter	....	....
14. happen	....	....
15. hum	....	....
16. level	....	....
17. quarrel	....	....
18. rub	....	....
19. signal	....	....
20. retreat	....	....

EXERCISE 4.

By adding the various endings, make new words. In some instances, the final consonant of the original word will be doubled. When in doubt, refer to the rules about doubling final consonants.

EXAMPLES:

Form an adjective of the word *woman* by adding *ish*.

Word	*Suffix*	*New Word*
woman	ish	womanish

1. Form an adjective of *wit* by adding *y*. ....

2. Form a noun from the verb *spin* by adding *er*. ....

3. Form a noun from the noun *blot* by adding *er*. ....

4. Form a noun by adding *er* to *design*. ....

5. Form an adjective by adding *ical* to *quiz*. ....

6. Form a noun by adding *er* to *shut*.   . . . .

7. Form a noun by adding *er* to *slip*.   . . . .

8. Form a noun by adding *eer* to *profit*.   . . . .

9. Form a noun by adding *ing* to *meet*.   . . . .

10. Form a noun by adding *er* to *dry*.   . . . .

11. Add *able* to *inhabit* to form an adjective.   . . . .

12. Add *er* to *toil* to form a noun.   . . . .

13. Add *er* to *put* to form a noun.   . . . .

14. Add *ment* to *develop* to form a noun.   . . . .

15. Add *ment* to *defer* to form a noun.   . . . .

16. Add *er* to *rub* to form a noun.   . . . .

17. Add *er* to *develop* to form a noun.   . . . .

18. Make the feminine of *god*.   . . . .

19. Name the man who sells you drugs.   . . . .

20. Add *er* to *trap* to form a noun.   . . . .

Rules For Spelling: The Final Y

THE FINAL Y

Why should the final Y cause so much trouble? Two simple rules will take care of all such words. Notice these words:

Singular	Plural
abb(ey)	abbeys
journ(ey)	journeys
monk(ey)	monkeys

THE Y PRECEDED BY A VOWEL

▶ RULE 1

The final Y following a vowel remains Y when suffixes are added.

These suffixes may be:

1. The letter *s* to form the plural.

EXAMPLES:

alley + S = alleys
attorney + S = attorneys
chimney + S = chimneys
donkey + S = donkeys

medley + S = medleys
pulley + S = pulleys
trolley + S = trolleys
valley + S = valleys
volley + S = volleys

2. The suffix *ing* or *ed*

EXAMPLES:

allay + ED = allayed; + ING = allaying
annoy + ED = annoyed; + ING = annoying
buy   + ING = buying

3. The suffix *er* meaning *one who.*

EXAMPLES:

buy + ER = buyer
employ + ER = employer

4. The suffix *ance*

EXAMPLE:

convey + ANCE = conveyance
Can you add other words?

5. The suffix *al*

EXAMPLE:

portray + AL = portrayal

EXERCISE 1.

Spell the following words correctly.

1. *tourney* in plural   . . . .
2. The past tense of *allay*.   . . . .
3. The past tense of *volley*.   . . . .
4. *alley* in plural.   . . . .
5. Past tense of *survey*.   . . . .
6. Present participle of *portray*. . . . .

7. Past tense of *journey*.   . . . .
8. Past tense of *relay*.   . . . .
9. Plural of *delay*.   . . . .
10. Past tense of *parlay*.   . . . .

THE Y PRECEDED BY A CONSONANT

So far we have studied the final Y preceded by a vowel. This did NOT CHANGE when a suffix was added. (*enjoy* + *ING* = *enjoying*).

▶ *RULE 2*

When a consonant precedes the Y the Y changes to *I* when suffixes are added.

KINDS OF SUFFIXES

1. The plural of the noun formed in ES.

EXAMPLES:

ally + ES = allies
enemy + ES = enemies
salary + ES = salaries
tragedy + ES = tragedies

2. The verb form with he, she, or it, formed by adding *es*, or *ed*.

EXAMPLES:

carry + ES = carries;   + ED = carried
dignify + ES = dignifies; + ED = dignified
marry + ES = marries;   + ED = married

3. Making an adjective by adding *ful*.

EXAMPLES:

beauty + FUL = beautiful
mercy + FUL = merciful
pity + FUL = pitiful

4. Making a noun by adding *ness*.

EXAMPLES:

busy + NESS = business
cozy + NESS = coziness
icy + NESS = iciness

5. Making an adverb by adding *ly*.

EXAMPLES:

airy + LY = airily
angry + LY = angrily
busy + LY = busily
clumsy + LY = clumsily

6. There is only one case in which the Y is retained. This is before *ing*.

EXAMPLES:

carry + ING = carrYing
copy + ING = copYing

EXERCISE 2

In the space to the right put C if the spelling is correct. If it is incorrect, write the proper spelling.

1. merciful ....
2. beautiful ....
3. cozily ....
4. attornies ....
5. valleys ....
6. surveyor ....
7. portraying ....
8. pitying ....
9. busied ....
10. icyly ....

EXERCISE 3

Write the correct spelling of the following words all of which end in final Y before adding a suffix.

1. pretty + ness   . . . .
2. petty + ness   . . . .
3. steady + ing   . . . .
4. ready + ed   . . . .
5. bully + s   . . . .
6. airy + ness   . . . .
7. pity + ed   . . . .
8. tally + ing   . . . .
9. buy + er   . . . .
10. duty + ful   . . . .
11. ready + ness   . . . .
12. carry + ed   . . . .
13. hurry + ing   . . . .
14. copy + er   . . . .
15. sloppy + ness   . . . .
16. lively + hood   . . . .
17. duty + ful   . . . .

▶ *CAUTION!*

When adding the present participle to verbs ending in Y, do not change the Y.

EXAMPLES:

Word	*+ ING*	*Present Participle*
accompany	+ ing	accompanying
bury	+ ing	burying
hurry	+ ing	hurrying
study	+ ing	studying
worry	+ ing	worrying

Why do you spell it *burial?*

Rules For Spelling: Farewell To The Final E

FAREWELL TO FINAL *E*

As you know, English has five *vowels:* A, E, I, O, U. The other letters are called *consonants.* Very often a consonant or group of consonants is added to a word and we get a second word. For example, let us consider the letters *ry.* Add these to the following nouns (names of persons, places, acts, or things).

chemist	(one who analyzes things)
chemistry	(the science of matter)
forest	(the collection of trees)
forestry	(the study of care of forests)
peasant	(worker of the soil)
peasantry	(the group of peasants)
mimic	(one who imitates another)
mimicry	(the art of imitation)

You see that no change occurs in spelling. You simply add the final element to a familiar word and you get a second word of a different meaning.

There are many endings of this character. If you remembered these endings and also that they don't change the spelling of the original word, you would find many apparently strange words really old friends with new attachments.

EXERCISE 1

Write the following words correctly by adding the suffix indicated:

1. pleasant + ry   . . . .
2. artist + ry   . . . .
3. portrait + ure   . . . .
4. clock + wise   . . . .
5. rocket + ry   . . . .
6. sophist + ry   . . . .
7. nation + ality   . . . .
8. person + ality   . . . .
9. dialectic + al   . . . .
10. practical + ity   . . . .

Few writers have any trouble in spelling words with added parts such as have just been described. But when a silent *E* occurs at the end of a word, problems arise. When should you retain the silent *E* and when should you drop it?

▶ RULE

Drop the E before an E (or A, I, O, U)

An additional part is called a suffix. If it begins with *a, e, i, o, u,* then drop the final silent *E* preceding the suffix.

Now some suffixes are:

able	ence
ed	ance
er	ing
est	ous

EXAMPLES:

Dropping the final *E* before *er:*

large + ER = largEr
love + ER = lovEr
live + ER = livEr

Dropping the final *E* before *est:*

large + EST = largEst
die + EST = (thou) diest

Dropping the final *E* before *able:*

love + ABLE = lovable
imagine + ABLE = imaginable
advise + ABLE = advisable

Dropping the final *E* before *ing:*

come + ING = coming
receive + ING = receiving
ache + ING = aching

Since many mistakes are made with the *ing* words, the following list is added. It contains some of your most useful words.

advise	whine	argue
advising	whining	arguing
dine	write	surprise
dining	writing	surprising
lose	shine	owe
losing	shining	owing
fascinate	oblige	purchase
fascinating	obliging	purchasing

become	judge	pursue
becoming	judging	pursuing
use	choose	
using	choosing	

Now try to build words for yourself. If you spell these newly-fashioned words correctly the first time you write them, you will always write them correctly.

EXAMPLES:

love + ABLE = lovable
love + ER = lover
love + ED = loved
love + ING = loving

Build similar words using these verbs to start with: *dine, use, write, move, rise.*

Dropping final *E* before OUS

The suffix *ous* is frequently added to a verb to make an adjective which always has the meaning, *full of.*

EXAMPLE:

desire + OUS = desirous

Sometimes the suffix OUS is added to a noun. Again an adjective results also meaning, *full of.*

EXAMPLE:

pore + OUS = porous; full of pores.

Dropping final *E* before ITY

The suffix ITY may be added to an adjective to form a noun. The final *E* before the suffix disappears.

EXAMPLE:

divine + ITY = divinity

The same thing happens with these words:

austere	extreme	immense
auster + ity	extrem + ity	immens + ity
dense	facile	intense
dens + ity	facil + ity	intens + ity
docile	grave	oblique
docil + ity	grav + ity	obliqu + ity
opportune	passive	rare
opportun + ity	passiv + ity	rar + ity
scarce	sincere	suave
scarc + ity	sincer + ity	suav + ity

EXERCISE 2

Form new words by spelling the following:

1. revere + ing ....
2. love + ly ....
3. purchase + able ....
4. extreme + ly ....
5. pleasure + able ....
6. large + ly ....
7. nudge + ed ....
8. state + ed ....
9. fete + ed ....
10. fine + ed ....
11. dive + ing ....
12. shove + ed ....
13. devise + ing ....
14. deceive + ed ....
15. relieve + ing ....
16. procrastinate + ing ....
17. imagine + ed ....
18. besiege + ed ....
19. receive + ing ....

There are some exceptions, but you can find a good reason for each of them.

Verbs ending in *oe* (canoe) retain the E to preserve the pronunciation.

EXAMPLES:

canoeing, hoeing, shoeing, toeing.

Dye and *singe* retain the E to differentiate the word from *die* and *sing*

EXAMPLES:

dyeing (one's hair)
dying (absence of life)
singeing (one's hair)
singing (a song)

EXERCISE 3

Form the present participle (+ ing) and the past participle (+ ed) of the following verbs.

EXAMPLE:

Word	Present Participle	Past Participle
argue	arguing	argued
1. benefit	. . . .	. . . .
2. commit	. . . .	. . . .
3. lure	. . . .	. . . .
4. refer	. . . .	. . . .
5. pine	. . . .	. . . .
6. elevate	. . . .	. . . .
7. propel	. . . .	. . . .
8. fit	. . . .	. . . .
9. recur	. . . .	. . . .
10. remit	. . . .	. . . .
11. open	. . . .	. . . .
12. club	. . . .	. . . .

13. plunge . . . .
14. singe . . . .
15. pursue . . . .
16. scare . . . .
17. throb . . . .
18. trot . . . .
19. use . . . .
20. whip . . . .

RETAIN FINAL *E*

The final *E* is retained when the suffix begins with a consonant (one of the letters remaining after the vowels *a,e,i,o,u* are removed).

Several suffixes begin with consonants.

Adding the suffix NESS

Examine the following words which all belong in this class:

acute	complete	genuine
acute NESS	complete NESS	genuine NESS
appropriate	expensive	large
appropriate NESS	expensive NESS	large NESS
vague	coarse	fierce
vague NESS	coarse NESS	fierce NESS
remote	like	polite
remote NESS	like NESS	polite NESS
white	rude	wide
white NESS	rude NESS	wide NESS

Add NESS to the following words ending in silent *E*, being sure to retain the *E*:

trite   stale

Adding the suffix MENT

What was said about the effect of NESS upon final silent *E* is true for *MENT*.

EXAMPLE:

state + MENT = statement

Examine the following words which are all formed the same way:

achieve	amuse	discourage
achieveMENT	amuseMENT	discourageMENT
advance	arrange	enforce
advanceMENT	arrangeMENT	enforceMENT
advertise	atone	engage
advertiseMENT	atoneMENT	engageMENT
amaze	commence	excite
amazeMENT	commenceMENT	exciteMENT
manage	move	require
manageMENT	moveMENT	requireMENT

The spelling of the following words will now be clear to you.

abateMENT	(from abate)
encourageMENT	(from encourage)
postponeMENT	(from postpone)

Adding the suffix FUL

Since the suffix *FUL* begins with a consonant, the silent *E* before it is retained.

EXAMPLE:

use + FUL = useful

The following words belong to this division:

care	tune
careFUL	tuneFUL
revenge	resource
revengeFUL	resourceFUL
taste	remorse
tasteFUL	remorseFUL
grace	hate
graceFUL	hateFUL
disgrace	shame
disgraceFUL	shameFUL

Adding the suffix LESS

Again the silent *E* is preserved because the suffix begins with the consonant *l*.

age	grace	sense	taste
ageLESS	graceLESS	senseLESS	tasteLESS
care	guide	shape	voice
careLESS	guideLESS	shapeLESS	voiceLESS
shame	tongue	cease	name
shameLESS	tongueLESS	ceaseLESS	nameLESS
change	noise	smoke	use
changeLESS	noiseLESS	smokeLESS	useLESS

A few tough cases:

When the word ends in double *e*, the final *E* is not dropped. This happens in order to retain the same pronunciation. Notice the word families below:

agree	see
agreeABLE	seeABLE
agreeING	seeING
agreeMENT	

Words ending in OE retain the final *E*

canoe	shoe
canoeING	shoeMAKER
woe	shoeSTRING
woeFUL	shoeING
woeBEGONE	hoe
	hoeING

Some Exceptions

Due, true, whole, drop the *e* before *ly*—duly, truly, wholly.

Some words ending in *E*, drop the *E* before *ment* or *ful*. Argument is an instance, as is awful (from *awe*). Why does *wise* drop the *E* in forming wisdom?

Words ending in *CE* or *GE* will retain the final *E* before a suffix beginning with a vowel. This is necessary to keep the soft pronunciation.

notice	change	outrage
noticeABLE	changeABLE	outrageOUS
service	courage	advantage
serviceABLE	courageOUS	advantageOUS

The reverse condition exists with certain words which would lose their hard pronunciation of certain consonants unless a *k* is added before a suffix beginning with *e, i,* or *y* (used as vowel).

EXAMPLE:

mimic + ing = mimicing would not be pronounced with the hard *c* (= to k). Hence the *k* is inserted between the final *c* and the beginning vowel of the suffix.

colic	colicky	
frolic	frolicking	frolicked

mimic	mimicking	mimicked
panic	panicking	panicked
picnic	picnicking	picnicked
traffic	trafficking	trafficked

Explain why this is not done for *frolicsome* or *panic-stricken* or *traffic-cop*.

EXERCISE 4

Try your hand at spelling these words containing the final *E* and a suffix.

1. agree	+ MENT =	. . . .
2. amuse	+ MENT =	. . . .
3. care	+ FUL =	. . . .
4. canoe	+ ING =	. . . .
5. come	+ ING =	. . . .
6. disagree	+ ABLE =	. . . .
7. engage	+ MENT =	. . . .
8. excite	+ MENT =	. . . .
9. immense	+ ITY =	. . . .
10. like	+ LY =	. . . .
11. safe	+ TY =	. . . .
12. sense	+ LESS =	. . . .
13. shine	+ ING =	. . . .
14. enlarge	+ MENT =	. . . .
15. entice	+ ING =	. . . .
16. perceive	+ ED =	. . . .
17. escape	+ ING =	. . . .
18. discharge	+ ED =	. . . .
19. relieve	+ ING =	. . . .
20. contrive	+ ANCE =	. . . .

EXERCISE 5

Have some one read the following sentences from dictation as you spell the words correctly. There will be many examples of dropping or retaining the final *E*.

1. While they were *staring* at the stars, they saw something *stirring* in the bushes.

2. It takes much *planning* to build a house *preferred* by others.

3. The *cannery* used plenty of *cane* sugar with such fruits as *pineapples* and peaches.

4. Dressed *sloppily,* the tramps *plodded* along wearily on the *pitted* country road.

5. By using *scraps* of food, the cook managed to scrape together a fair meal after the *scrapping* of the parents was over.

6. The little *moppet* sat *moping* in her little chair while the mother *mopped* up the food which was lying *sloppily* on the floor.

7. After we *refused* to have anything to do with her, the discharged maid *fumed* and *fussed effusively* and finally stamped out of the room.

8. By *dotting* your *i*'s and *crossing* your *t*'s you can take a small step toward *better spelling.*

9. While a troop of cavalry was *ridding* the woods of the stragglers, a second troop was *riding* into the village.

10. As the giant airliner *hopped* off, my parents were *praying* and *hoping* that all would go well.

EXERCISE 6

Each of the following words has an error in the dropping or retention of final E. Make the correction in the space to the right.

1. scarcly   . . . .
2. vengance   . . . .
3. truely   . . . .
4. tastey   . . . .
5. noticable   . . . .
6. changable   . . . .
7. perspireing   . . . .
8. retireing   . . . .
9. aweful   . . . .
10. wisedom   . . . .
11. assureance   . . . .
12. insureance   . . . .
13. outragous   . . . .
14. servicable   . . . .
15. couragous   . . . .
16. gorgous   . . . .
17. pronouncable   . . . .

Rules For Spelling: IE And EI

The June 22, 1957 *Saturday Review of Literature* contained the following story:

A neophyte copy editor in a large advertising agency was slowly going out of his mind because his copy chief was constantly taking a small slip of paper from his breast pocket, looking at it, leering, then putting it back. After watching this for months he managed one day, when the copy chief was taking a nap, to steal the secret paper from the jacket in back of the chief's chair. He opened the slip of paper with trembling hands.

It read.

"*I* before *E* except after *C*"[1]

IE AND EI

You may be relieved when you receive this information. Although a great deal of mischief has been caused by people who were confused about the use of *IE* or *EI*, there is a simple rule that will take care of all cases.

---

[1] Reprinted by permission of *Saturday Review of Literature*.

▶ *LEARN THIS RULE!*

Put i before e,
Except after c,
Or when sounded like *a*,
As in *neighbor* and *weigh*;
And except *seize* and *seizure*
And also *leisure*,
Weird, height, and *either,*
Forfeit and *neither.*

▶ *REMEMBER!*

When the two letters *IE* or *EI* are sounded like ē,
then: It is *i* before *e* except after *c*. The exceptions of words that
have the ē sound are in the sentence:

Did either or neither financier seize a weird species
of leisure?

You may remember the word *Celia,* or *Alice,* which
will help you for the *L* and *C*.

Examine the list below.

IE

bel*ie*f	p*ie*ce
f*ie*ld	pr*ie*st
misch*ie*f	rel*ie*ve
y*ie*ld	

Notice that in no case does a *C* precede the *IE*.
It is always a letter other than *C*.

Now examine the additional list:

ach*ie*ve	befr*ie*nd	f*ie*f	fr*ie*ze	handkerch*ie*f
aggr*ie*ve	bel*ie*ve	f*ie*nd	front*ie*r	hyg*ie*ne
al*ie*n	bes*ie*ge	f*ie*rce	gr*ie*f	interv*ie*w

chief	bier	fiery	grievance	lief
lien	brief	friend	grieve	liege
niece	lieu	mien	mischief	mischievous
quiet	piebald	pied	pierce	piety
review	relief	relieve	reprieve	retrieve
siege	series	shield	shriek	shrieve
tier	sienna	sieve	thief	thievery
	view	wield	yield	

EXERCISE 1

Study the list above carefully; notice that never does a *c* precede the *IE*. Any other letter in the alphabet may do so, but not the *c*. Write each word once, one word to a line; pronounce it; then write it once in a sentence; follow this scheme.

Word	Pronounce	Sentence
achieve	a chēē v	I hope to achieve my goal.

EXERCISE 2

When you feel certain that you know the preceding words, copy and fill in the missing letters in the following:

1. aggr _ _ ve
2. br _ _ f
3. fr _ _ nd
4. gr _ _ ve
5. front _ _ r
6. misch _ _ f
7. sh _ _ ld
8. shr _ _ k
9. w _ _ ld
10. for _ _ gn
11. rel _ _ ve
12. l _ _ sure
13. handkerch _ _ f
14. rec _ _ pt
15. s _ _ ze
16. perc _ _ ve
17. gr _ _ f
18. n _ _ ce
19. conc _ _ ve
20. v _ _ l

A FEW ASSOCIATIONS

Sometimes it will help you to form words into certain groups. Thus if you associate the words with chief you will get

CHIEF

handker*chief* mis*chief* mis*chiev*ous

If you remember the spelling of *chief* (and few ever forget it), the spelling of the other three is easy for you.

Think of field and shield; belief, believe, relief, relieve, brief, reprieve, tier, frontier.

Now we can master the other combinations. Study the following words:

EI

dec*ei*t
per*cei*ve   *ei* follows c
re*cei*ve

fr*ei*ght
v*ei*l   *ei* because the sound is $\bar{a}$ as in *hay*
n*ei*gh

either
height
leisure
forfeit
neither   special cases
seize
weird
seizure

Read this list carefully and notice that in each case the *EI* follows *c*.

ce*i*ling   dece*i*tful
conce*i*t   dece*i*ve
conce*i*ted   rece*i*pt
conce*i*ve   rece*i*ve

The following list has the *EI* because it sounds like ā in *bay*.

deign	rein	veil
heir	skein	vein
inveigh	sleigh	weigh
inveigle	surveillance	weight
reign	their	

You have noticed that in *reign*, there is the sound of ā. Although in *foreign, sovereign* and *sovereignty* the *eign* is not sounded as ā, it will help you to associate these four words.

EXAMPLE:

The foreign sovereign resigned when his sovereignty was disputed.

THE SPECIAL CASES

EXAMPLE:

The final *feit* is pronounced *fit*.

forfeit
counterfeit
surfeit

EXAMPLE:

These are pronounced ī as *kite*. Be sure to put the *e* in.

height
sleight

EXAMPLE:

A few words have *cie*, but in all cases the *c* is pronounced as sh.

ancient	deficient	glacier	species
conscience	efficient	proficient	sufficient

EXERCISE 3

As a final test of your skill, have someone dictate the following paragraph to you.

A thief tried to deceive a priest. The priest was a friendly soul, but such mischief was beyond belief. Rather than forfeit the night's receipts, he feigned weakness. He waited for an opportunity to seize his attacker and because of his superior height was able to overpower his enemy.

Rules For Spelling: Plurals Of Nouns

PLURALS OF NOUNS

Most English nouns add S to form the plural.

EXAMPLES:

cat + S = cats
hat + S = hats
house + S = houses

A number of nouns ending in long ō add ES.

▶ *LEARN THIS*
  ENTIRE LIST!

buffalo ES	motto ES
calico ES	negro ES
cargo ES	potato ES
desperado ES	tomato ES
domino ES	torpedo ES
echo ES	veto ES
embargo ES	virago ES
hero ES	volcano ES
mosquito ES	

A few nouns ending in ō, add only an S.

▶ *REMEMBER THEM*
BY GROUPS!

MUSIC
altos
sopranos
contraltos   all are borrowed from Italian
pianos
solos

CIRCULAR APPEARANCE
dynamos   silos
cameos

Certain nouns ending in *f* or *fe* form the plural by changing *f* to *v* and adding S or ES. Each word must be studied individually.

Singular	*Plural*
beef	beeves
calf	calves
elf	elves
knife	knives
leaf	leaves
life	lives
loaf	loaves
sheaf	sheaves
thief	thieves
wife	wives
wolf	wolves

These words may be learned in groups according to the sound of the vowel before the *f*.

ē͞e Sound
beef	beeves
leaf	leaves

sheaf	sheaves
thief	thieves

ī Sound

knife	knives
life	lives
wife	wives

el Sound

elf	elves
self	selves
shelf	shelves

Following are groups of words ending in *f* which add only S for the plural.

IEF

belief	beliefs
brief	briefs
chief	chiefs
grief	griefs
handkerchief	handkerchiefs

OOF

hoof	hoofs (rarely hooves)
proof	proofs
roof	roofs

RF

dwarf	dwarfs
scarf	scarfs (or scarves)
turf	turfs
wharf	wharfs (or wharves)

EXERCISE 1

Write plurals for the following words:

1. reproof   . . . .
2. reprieve   . . . .
3. sieve   . . . .
4. halo   . . . .
5. gulf   . . . .
6. coif   . . . .
7. albino   . . . .
8. shelf   . . . .
9. puff   . . . .
10. muff   . . . .
11. slough   . . . .
12. basso   . . . .
13. mambo   . . . .
14. surf   . . . .
15. trough   . . . .
16. stiletto   . . . .
17. sheaf   . . . .
18. radio   . . . .
19. calf   . . . .
20. sylph   . . . .

Words ending in *y* preceded by a vowel form their plural by adding S.

Study this list.

day	days
boy	boys
monkey	monkeys
valley	valleys
volley	volleys

These add only S because a vowel precedes the *y*.

EXERCISE 2

Write the plurals of these words:

1. abbey ....
2. alley ....
3. attorney ....
4. buoy ....
5. chimney ....
6. donkey ....
7. journey ....
8. key ....
9. pulley ....
10. turkey ....

When the final *y* is preceded by a consonant the *y* changes to *i* and ES is added to form the plural.

Study this list.

academy	academies
actuary	actuaries
ally	allies
army	armies
caddy	caddies
cry	cries

Compound nouns add S or ES to only the principal word to form the plural.

In the *in-law* series, the principal word is son, brother, etc.

EXAMPLES:
brothers-in-law
mothers-in-law

A few compound words are practically single words and add the S at the end. This explains such cases as

> spoonfuls
> cupfuls
> bowlfuls
> handfuls

A long time ago the English language had quite a list of words whose plurals ended not in S but in EN. Only a few are left today, but they never give any trouble because they are learned in the very early grades of school. Other variations follow:

child	children
brother	brethren (of a congregation)
ox	oxen
foot	feet
tooth	teeth
goose	geese
cannon	cannon (or S)
deer	deer
sheep	sheep
swine	swine

The animals:

| louse | lice |
| mouse | mice |

The sexes:

| man | men |
| woman | women |

From French:

| madam | mesdames |
| monsieur | messieurs |

NAMES OF PEOPLE

As a general rule add S to form the plural:

EXAMPLES:

All the Johns in the school.
All the Jennys in this class.

LETTERS, SIGNS, FIGURES

These form their plural by adding 's.

EXAMPLES:

Cross your t's
Mind your P's and Q's
Underline the 3's in the line.

FOREIGN WORDS

Foreign words act differently when their plurals are formed. Since many of these foreign plurals are from the Latin, the Latin plurals are used.

Many Latin words ending in *us* form their plural by changing the *us* to *i*. The most familiar of such words is

alumnus (a graduate of a school)
alumni (graduates)

Others in this group are:

fungus	fungi
focus	foci
radius	radii
bacillus	bacilli
terminus	termini

Some Latin words ending in *um* change it to *a* to form the plural. A familiar word to us is *datum, data* (the facts in the case).

Familiar UM—A Words

medium	media (means of doing things)
addendum	addenda (things added to a book or program)
bacterium	bacteria
candelabrum	candelabra
curriculum	curricula
desideratum	desiderata
erratum	errata
maximum	maxima
memorandum	memoranda
minimum	minima
stadium	stadia
stratum	strata

Latin has a group of nouns ending in *is* singular, *es* plural. A familiar case is *crisis, crises.*

EXAMPLES:

amanuensis	amanuenses (one who takes down your writing)
analysis	analyses
antithesis	antitheses (opposite)
axis	axes (centèr)
ellipsis	ellipses
hypothesis	hypotheses (assumption)
oasis	oases
parenthesis	parentheses
synopsis	synopses

The Greek language has given us a few plurals.
These are from the ancient Greeks.

automaton   automata (mechanical figures
         working by themselves)
criterion   criteria (standard of judg-
         ment)

From the French have come these strange plurals:

beau   beaux (or beaus)
tableau   tableaux (or tableaus)
chateau   chateaux
portmanteau   portmanteaux (or portmanteaus)

These familiar words are all Italian plural forms:

spaghetti
confetti
banditti
ravioli

EXERCISE 3
Plurals of nouns.
Form the plurals of the following nouns:

1. t   . . . .
2. Mary   . . . .
3. anniversary . . . .
4. dromedary . . . .
5. kerchief   . . . .
6. 4   . . . .
7. court-martial . . . .
8. lieutenant colonel . . . .
9. bay   . . . .
10. tray   . . . .

11. flurry   . . . .
12. sulky   . . . .
13. surrey   . . . .
14. inequity   . . . .
15. satellite   . . . .
16. functionary   . . . .
17. avocado   . . . .
18. dynamo   . . . .

EXERCISE 4

Have someone dictate the following passage containing many singular nouns for which you will write the plurals.

Mother sent Mary to the Grand Union to purchase some *grocery* _____ for the long week end. Among the *thing* _____ she wanted to obtain were: *tomato* _____, *potato* _____, and *avocado* _____. She also asked for several *quart* _____ of milk, two *pound* _____ of butter, several *piece* _____ of cake, and a pound of caramel-filled *chocolate* _____.

After making these and several other *purchase* _____, Mary started to return home. Several interesting *adventure* _____ occurred to her on the way. She met her friend Nancy who was one of the best *soprano* _____ in the church choir. Mary herself was usually placed among the *alto* _____. After wandering up and down several narrow *alley* _____, she ended one of the most interesting *journey* _____ by finding a bundle of *key* _____, which she had lost several *day* _____ before. Such *event* _____ happen too seldom, and Mary will not forget this for a long time.

Use Of The Apostrophe

The apostrophe has several important uses in correct spelling. Study the following:

Use the apostrophe to indicate a lost vowel.
EXAMPLES:

do not = don't
can not = can't
could not = couldn't
you are = you're
they are = they're

Most frequently the apostrophe is used to show possession. A singular noun not ending in *s* adds *'s*.
EXAMPLES:

The hat of the girl = the girl's hat
The rights of the man = the man's rights

Add *'s* to a singular noun which ends in *s* or an s-sound if a new syllable is formed by pronouncing the possessive.
EXAMPLES:

The hair of the actress = the actress's hair
The daughter of the boss = the boss's daughter

To avoid the repetition of the s-sound, just add the apostrophe.

EXAMPLE:

> for mildness' sake

To show possession with a plural noun, add *'s* if the noun does not end in *s*.

EXAMPLES:

> men's hosiery
> women's hats
> children's shoes

If the plural ends in *s* (as most nouns do) add only the apostrophe.

EXAMPLES:

> the doctors' fees
> the dentists' conference
> the teachers' demands

To show possession of a singular proper noun not ending in *s*, add *'s*.

EXAMPLES:

> Mr. Mann's library
> Miss Smith's dog
> Dr. Levitt's office

When the proper noun ends in *s* and has only one syllable, add *'s*.

EXAMPLES:

> Alger Hiss's case
> Rudolf Hess's escape

When the proper noun ending in *s* has two or more syllables, add only the apostrophe.

EXAMPLES:

>Mr. Dickens' readings
>Roger Williams' expulsion

Use the same rule for indefinite pronouns.

EXAMPLES:

>One's honor is at stake. (singular)
>The others' hats were soiled while ours were clean. (plural)

DOUBLE OWNERSHIP

When you wish to indicate ownership by two or more persons, use the apostrophe *only* for the last.

EXAMPLES:

>Lewis and Clark's Expedition
>Jim and Joe's locker
>Smith, Kline and French's drugs

▶ *NOTE!*

If you are talking about separate ownership, you use the apostrophe after each noun.

EXAMPLE:

>The President's and Secretary of State's reports
>This means there were two reports,
>one by each officer.

COMPOUND NOUNS

The apostrophe is used only after the last noun in the compound.

EXAMPLES:

>my mother-in-law's house
>the man-of-war's deck

PERSONAL PRONOUNS

These never use the apostrophe for their possessive case.

EXAMPLE:

his, hers, its, ours, theirs

▶ *NOTE!*

Be especially careful with *whose*. What is the difference between

Whose house is this?

and

Who's there?

▶ *REMEMBER!*

The apostrophe means "belonging to whatever immediately precedes it," except when it is used to indicate a lost vowel.

children's — belonging to children

men's — belonging to men

boss's — belonging to a single boss

bosses' — belonging to more than one boss

EXERCISE 1.

Rewrite the following phrases in such a way as to use the apostrophe in showing possession:

1. The hat of the young girl

   . . . .

2. The votes of the men

   . . . .

3. The styles of the ladies

   . . . .

4. The paws of the cats

. . . .

5. The decorations of the sailors

. . . .

6. The hat of the professor

. . . .

7. A shoe of a woman

. . . .

8. The voice of the soprano

. . . .

9. The tail of the dog

. . . .

Add the apostrophe in the following sentences to show omission of a letter.

10. They do not vote often. . . . .

11. We have not any money. . . . .

12. The allies could not agree on the campaign. . . . .

13. You are always late. . . . .

14. They can not always win. . . . .

15. It is too late to go now. . . . .

16. Let us wait a little longer. . . . .

17. We would not have acted so if we were not hungry. . . . .

Capital Letters

BEGIN WITH A CAPITAL LETTER

1. The first word of a sentence.
2. The first word of a quoted sentence.
3. The first word of a line of poetry.
4. The first word, and important words, in titles of books or themes.
5. Proper nouns.
6. The words I and O in direct address.

PROPER NOUNS

Capitalize	*Do not capitalize*
Proper Names	Words that are not a specific name
Sioux City	our high school
Eastern District High School	the cold stream
State Legislature	
United Nations	
Definite place names	Point of the compass
the North vs. the South	four degrees north

Definite events

May Day
War of 1870

The names of the seasons

spring   autumn
summer   winter

Races, Languages

German
Hindu
French

Studies other than languages

chemistry
biology

Titles

Uncle Don
Dr. Jones

A title after a modifier

my uncle
a doctor
I have two brothers
my cousins arrived

Organizations: clubs, corporations, churches, departments, political parties

The Odd Fellows (club)
Bethlehem Steel Corporation
Methodist Episcopal Church
The Farmer-Labor Party

Deity and words associated with Deity

God
Christ
St. John
Scriptures

Trade names

Capitalize only the part of the trade name that differentiates it from all other brands.

Arrow shirt
Revlon's lotion

Family relationships

> Aunt
> Mother

In place of the person's name (especially in direct address)

> "Hurry up, Aunt!"
> "Yes, Mother, I'm hurrying!"

BOOKS, PLAYS, MUSIC

> ▶ *REMEMBER THIS*
> *RULE IN*
> *CAPITALIZING*
> *A TITLE!*

Don't cap the "caps." The last "cap" stands for

c — conjunctions (and, for)
a — articles (the, a, an)
p — (prepositions (of, to, for, from)

EXAMPLE:

Book:	Rose of the Rancho
Play:	The Way of the World
	Right You Are if You Think You Are
Music:	To a Wild Rose
	Pie in the Sky

EXERCISE 1.

Try your hand at capitalizing the words that need capitals.

1. We stopped at the hotel westover.
2. The buick cars are well advertised.
3. We celebrate decoration day.

4. the north side high school
5. We saw mutiny on the bounty.
6. They sang old french folk songs.
7. In english courts the bible is kissed.
8. Harriet Beecher Stowe's uncle Tom is know wherever the book is read.
9. They walked along fifth avenue.
10. Many people ask for washington coffee.
11. Our vacation to britain lasted six weeks.
12. Bard college is in new york.
13. the taming of the shrew is a play written b shakespeare.
14. My courses in college include mathematics english, and three years of french.
15. Last spring we visited aunt emily who lives ou west.

Prefix Confusion

The word *cross* is never misspelled. Yet *across* has had many spelling victims. Why? People forget that the prefix (in this word, *a*) is never doubled. Learn the following prefixes:

a + like = alike
a + round = around
a + mount = amount

dis + appoint = disappoint
dis + advantage = disadvantage
dis + able = disable

in + nate = innate
in + novate = innovate

mis + spell = misspell
mis + shapen = misshapen
mis + state = misstate

over + run = overrun
over + ride = override
over + rate = overrate

pro + fessional = professional
pro + duce = produce
pro + file = profile

re + arrange = rearrange
re + collect = recollect
re + commend = recommend

un + natural = unnatural
un + noticeable = unnoticeable
un + occupied = unoccupied

▶ *BE CAREFUL OF THE MEANINGS OF THE FOLLOWING PREFIXES !*

de = *down*	descend	to walk down
	demote	to put down
	destroy	to tear down
dis = *apart*	dismember	to tear limb from limb
	dissolve	to fall apart in a liquid
	disarm	to separate a soldier from his weapons
per = *through*	permeate	to penetrate
	perspire	to come through the pores of the skin
	persevere	to go through to the end
pre = *before*	precede	to go before
	predict	to tell beforehand
	prehistoric	before history

FURTHER EXERCISES IN LATIN PREFIXES

AB means *away* or *from* in Latin. *DUCT* means *lead* in Latin.

Put the two together, and you have *abduct,* to steal somebody away. Most words beginning with *AB* have the meaning *away* or *from.* This fact will not only help your spelling but will also enlarge your vocabulary.

▶ *EXAMINE THE*
FOLLOWING:

abhor	abdicate	abstain
abrupt	absent	absolve

ANTE means before

An *anteroom* is a room before another. The following words all have this prefix:

antediluvian   before the flood
ante-bellum   before the war
antechamber   a small room attached to a large one
antecedent   ancestor

ANTI means against

anti-vivisectionist
antiseptic   against poisoning
anti-noise campaign

CIRCUM means around

circumscribe   to write around
circumnavigate   to sail around
circumlocution   act of talking around the topic
rather than directly

DE signifies away, down, from

dethrone	decrease	deform
degrade	demerit	debar

INTER signifies among

interstate (commerce)   intersect   international
interfere   interrupt   intercollegiate
interview

NON means not. This prefix is quite familiar.

nonsense   nonconformist
nonentity   noncombatant

POST means behind or after

postpone   postscript (P.S.)
postgraduate   post-mortem

PRO means forward, before, instead of

procession   provide (to look forward)   promote
provisions   Providence

RE means back, again, against

refer (to bring back to the previous question)
retaliate (to fight back)
retract (to take back your statement)
repel (to hurl back)

SE means aside, apart

secede (to separate from the mother country)
secession   seclude   separate

SUB equals under

subway   subtract
subscribe (to write your name under the written
           material)

SUPER means above

superintendent superfluous supersede
superficial superstructure

TRANS means across

transcontinental (airway) transgressor
transfer translucent
transplant transient

Armed with a knowledge of these prefixes, you will understand and spell correctly at a glance many thousands of words.

EXERCISE 1

Try your skill in building your own words.
Take, for example, *scribe*, meaning a writer.

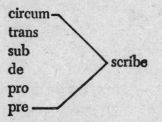

circum
trans
sub
de
pro
pre

scribe

Give the meaning of each.

EXERCISE 2

By adding the proper Latin prefixes to the following italicized words, spell the new formations correctly.

EXAMPLES:

not satisfied   dissatisfied
not legible   illegible

1. A *step* wrongly taken . . . .
2. not to *understand* . . . .
3. not *similar* . . . .
4. to *echo* again and again . . . .
5. below the *standard* . . . .
6. above the speed of sound . . . .
7. before the time of *Columbus* . . . .
8. he is against *imperialism* . . . .
9. one who *navigates* around the globe . . . .
10. complications after an *operation* . . . .

Some difficulties with the spelling of prefixes may be due to carelessness in pronunciation. Thus if you don't pronounce *prescription* properly, you may not spell the prefix with *pre*. The reverse error may come with a word like *per*spiration, in which the initial *per* may be misspelled.

Knowing the meaning of certain prefixes, as indicated earlier in this chapter, will help you to both know the meaning of the word and its spelling.

Per through

Word	*Meaning*
permeate	to penetrate through and through
perforate	to pierce through
perpetual	through the years
persist	to continue through a project
persecute	to follow through
perspective	to see through

Contrast these *per* words with *pre* words in which the meaning is *before*.

Word	*Meaning*
precocious	to develop earlier

prefer	to place before
prepare	to make ready beforehand
prejudice	a judgment before the evidence is in
prescribe	to write before

Contrast the *pre* and *per* words with those beginning with *pro*, which means *in front of* or *in behalf of*.

Word	Meaning
propose	to place before a group
prophecy	something stated before it happens
proceed	to move forward
proclaim	to shout before
produce	to bring forth
prognosis	to forecast the probable outcome of a disease

EXERCISE 3

Underline the correct spelling of the pairs of words in the following sentences:

1. The secret police (persecuted, presecuted) the prisoner.
2. Let us (preceed, proceed) with the trial.
3. This young bright child was obviously (precocious, percocious).
4. We must look at world affairs in the proper (perspective, prospective).
5. The patient asked the doctor to (proscribe, prescribe) something for his cough.
6. The illness was diagnosed as a (perforated, proferated) ulcer.
7. It costs a great deal to (perduce, produce) a musical comedy.
8. We must (persist, presist) in our efforts to find ways to peace.
9. Searching for the truth requires (perpetual, prepetual) effort.
10. Let us (propose, perpose) a toast.

Suffix Confusion

WORDS ENDING IN *ABLE, IBLE*

When you are able to add *able* and *ible* correctly, you have an ability that is to be envied. If you learn how to use *able* correctly, then *ably* and *ability* follow naturally.

With this particular spelling difficulty, the best advice is: *Observe Carefully*. There is no hard and set rule. But if you master a few key words, the others will come easily.

Consider some of our simplest words:

eat + able = eatable
laugh + able = laughable
comfort + able = comfortable

You will notice in the list that follows, our most familiar words add *-able* to form the adjective. This list contains most of the words in ordinary use:

talk + able
drink + able
read + able
unthink + able

Now study the words that end in *-ible*. You will notice that the words in the following group have a double *-ss* before the *-ible*.

accessible   admissible   compressible
irrepressible   possible   permissible
transmissible

Each of these words, except *possible* and *irrepressible*, you will notice, has a noun ending in *ion*. That is another sure way to recall their spelling.

accession   accessible
admission   admissible

Few writers make mistakes in spelling the noun *permission*, and you should not have difficulty with the adjective if you associate the suffix *-ion* with *ible*. How would you tell the spelling of a word like *kiss*? It ends in *iss*. But it has no noun in *-ion* (*kission*) and hence no ending in *-ible*, but has the form kiss*able*.

You can apply this *-ion -ible* test to many doubtful words, and you will be able to think of the correct form that way.

▶ *NOTICE!*

The following words all end in *ion*:

apprehension   coercion   corruption
combustion   comprehension   division
destruction   digestion   perception
expansion   extension   reprehension
perfection
reversion

Now the simple rule in all of these words is: Drop the *on* and add *ble*.

EXAMPLE:

apprehension — on = apprehensi + ble
This removes the whole problem of *a* or *i* in forming the suffix.
Practically all other adjectives ending in *ble* have *able*.

Adjectives which also end in *-ible* but do not have an *-ion* form can be remembered in this way: The *ible* is necessary to preserve the sound of soft *g* or *c*.

Thus the word *tangent* has the adjective *tangible,* because an *able* would change the pronunciation of *g* from its present *j* sound to the sound of *g* in *gum*. Other words in this class are:

dedu*cible*	produ*cible*	redu*cible*
condu*cible*	corri*gible*	incorri*gible*
eli*gible*	ineli*gible*	iras*cible*
intelli*gible*	invin*cible*	le*gible*

EXERCISE 1

Here is a list of words. Add *able* or *ible*. Be sure that you know all the reasons for adding *-ible*.

1. It follows double *ss* and comes from a noun ending in *sion* (permission).
2. It ends in *-ion* (coercion).
3. It keeps the *c* or *g* soft (deducible, eligible).

account	depend	market
avoid	detest	perish
comfort	discount	return
companion	fashion	review
credit	favor	season

Did you add *-able* to each of these? Then you were 100% correct. Now add *-able* or *-ible* to the roots of these words:

EXAMPLE:

abomination   abominable

commendation
admiration

conformation
appreciation
consideration
(Hint: consol *a* tion, consol *a* ble)

Did you add -*able* to the roots of each of these words? You were 100% correct. You can accept as a basic fact: a noun ending in -*ation* will have an adjective in -*able*.

As a final task, add the endings -*able*, or -*ible* to the roots of the following words:

EXAMPLE:

demonstration   demonstrable

derivation	exportation	notation
duration	habitation	refutation
estimation	imagination	separation
execration	irritation	taxation
	lamentation	toleration

You should add -*able* to the roots of each of the words.

EXERCISE 2

Have some one dictate the following passage which contains many words ending in the suffixes *ible* or *able*.

The prosecuting attorney protested that the evidence by the defendant about his *taxable* income was *inadmissible*. In the first place, it was not easily *accessible*. In the second place, although the evidence was originally *acceptable* in a lower court, the decisions in such courts are *reversible*.

The defendant's attorney objected that such reasoning was *unsupportable* and *intolerable* and that it was *reprehensible* on his opponent's part to bring up such a claim. The tension was increasing *perceptibly*. If this continued, the defending attorney might have to be ejected *forcibly*, or be *eligible* for disbarment. However, it took some time for the atmosphere to be cleared and the case proceeded to its *inevitable* conclusion.

WORDS ENDING IN *ANCE, ENCE*

There are no simple ways of learning when to add *ance* or *ence*. It is best to study each of the following lists, using the words as often as possible until you habitually spell them correctly.

common *ance, ant, ancy* words

abundant	ignorant
abundance	importance
acquaintance	important
appearance	inheritance
assistance	irrelevancy
assistant	irrelevant
balance	lieutenant
brilliance	maintenance
brilliancy	nuisance
brilliant	observance
clearance	observant
countenance	pendant
defendant	perseverance
descendant	pleasant
elegance	preponderant
elegant	remembrance
endurance	remonstrance
entrance	repentance
entrant	repentant
grievance	restaurant
guidance	sergeant
hindrance	significance
ignorance	significant

stimulant   tenant
tenancy   tolerance

common *ence, ent, ency* words

absence	dependence
absent	dependent
abstinence	difference
abstinent	different
adherence	diffidence
adherent	diffident
antecedent	diligence
apparent	diligent
audience	divergence
coherence	divergent
coherent	efficiency
coincidence	efficient
concurrence	eminence
concurrent	eminent
conference	essence
confidence	(essential)
confident	equivalent
conscience	excellence
consequence	excellent
consequent	existence
competence	existent
competent	experience
compliment (praise)	government
convenience	impertinence
convenient	impertinent
correspondence	imprudence
correspondent	imprudent
deference	independence
(deferential)	independent

indulgence
indulgent
inference
influence
(influential)
insistence
insolence
insolent
intelligence
intelligent
intermittent
magnificence
magnificent
occurrence
opponent
patent
patience
patient
penitence
penitent
permanence
permanent
persistence

persistent
pestilence
precedence
preference
presence
present
prominence
prominent
providence
provident
reference
repellent
reverence
reverent
residence
resident
sentence
sufficient
superintendent
tendency
violence
violent

WORDS ENDING IN *ENSE*

There are only a few words ending in *ense*

defense or defence (British)
expense
immense
offense or offence
pretense or pretence
suspense

EXERCISE 3

Insert *a* or *e* in the space indicated for the following words:

1. complim_nt
2. remembr_nce
3. consist_nt
4. superintend_nt
5. depend_nt
6. exist_nce
7. descend_nt
8. acquaint_nce
9. griev_nce
10. perman_nt
11. magnific_nt
12. brilli_nce
13. compl_mentary
14. conveni_nce
15. abund_nce
16. guid_nce
17. consci_nce
18. coincid_nce
19. appar_nt
20. consequ_ntial

THE ADVERBIAL SUFFIX *LY*

In forming adverbs from adjectives ending in *al*, simply add *ly* to the original word.

adjective + ly = adverb

EXAMPLE:

verbal + ly = verbally

EXERCISE 4

Form the adverbs of the following adjectives:

1. accidental
2. critical
3. elemental
4. equal
5. exceptional
6. final
7. general (adj.)
8. incidental
9. intentional
10. ironical
11. logical
12. mathematical
13. practical
14. professional
15. real
16. typical

17. usual   19. **global**
18. verbal

WORDS ENDING IN *ARY, ERY*

There are more than 300 words ending in *ary*. There are only two commonly used words ending in *ery:*

> cemetery   stationery

Perhaps it may help you to remember that in cemetery only *e*'s are used. Recall that station*ery* is used to write a lett*er*.

Some common words ending in *ary*

auxiliary
boundary
centenary
dictionary
elementary
evolutionary
honorary
imaginary
infirmary
library
revolutionary
secretary
secondary
tertiary
tributary
vocabulary
involuntary

WORDS ENDING IN *ISE, IZE*

There are no hard and fast rules to differentiate between the words ending in *ise* and *ize*. Perhaps the best procedure would be to master the list of *ise* words and then remember that all others are spelled *ize*.

advertisement
advise
adviser
arise
chastise
(chastisement)
compromise
demise
despise
disguise
enterprise
exercise

franchise
merchandise
revise
(revision)
supervise
(supervision)
surmise
surprise
reprise
(reprisal)

WORDS ENDING IN *IZE*

agonize
antagonize
authorize
(authorization)
baptize (but baptism)
burglarize
capsize
centralize
characterize
(characterization)
demoralize
dramatize
emphasize (but emphasis)
familiarize
fertilize
generalize

generalization
humanize
hypnotize
idolization
itemize
legitimatize
localize
modernize
neutralize
ostracize
patronize
pulverize
realize
recognize
solemnize
specialize

symbolize	terrorize
tantalize	visualize

In some instances the British spelling is *ise* instead of American *ize*.

EXAMPLES:

realise	criticise	penalise

There are only two words ending in *yze*:

analyze	paralyze

WORDS ENDING IN *OUS*

The suffix *ous* means *full of* and occasionally gives some people difficulties because they tend to add an *i*. Another difficulty may arise with nouns which end in *e* and then add *ous*. See page 52 for the rule.

The following words simply add *ous* to the noun to form the adjective:

Noun		*Suffix*		
danger	+	ous	=	dangerous
hazard	+	ous	=	hazardous
humor	+	ous	=	humorous
libel	+	ous	=	libelous
marvel	+	ous	=	marvelous
moment	+	ous	=	momentous
mountain	+	ous	=	mountainous
murder	+	ous	=	murderous
peril	+	ous	=	perilous
poison	+	ous	=	poisonous
riot	+	ous	=	riotous
slander	+	ous	=	slanderous

The following words are based on nouns which ended in *e*. Because the suffix begins with a vowel, the final *e* is dropped.

adventure	+	ous	=	adventurous
analogue	+	ous	=	analogous
desire	+	ous	=	desirous
trouble	+	ous	=	troublous

The following words are based on nouns ending in *f*, which changed to *v* when the *ous* was added:

grief	+	ous	=	grievous
mischief	+	ous	=	mischievous

Be especially careful not to insert an *i* which was never at the end of the word.

Occasionally the final *e* is retained before *ous* for phonetic reasons, as has been explained on page 52. Such words are:

courage	+	ous	=	courageous
advantage	+	ous	=	advantageous
outrage	+	ous	=	outrageous

WORDS ENDING IN Y PLUS *OUS*

Common sense will tell us that when *beauty* adds *ous*, the sound would remain. In order to prevent the sound of *sh* from entering (as would happen with *tio*), the *y* is dropped and an *e* is added, as in:

beauty	+	ous	=	beauteous
bounty	+	ous	=	bounteous
duty	+	ous	=	duteous
pity	+	ous	=	piteous
plenty	+	ous	=	plenteous

EXERCISE 5

Write the correct adjectives of the following nouns by adding the suffixes indicated.

1. advantage   (ous)   . . . .
2. courage   (ous)   . . . .
3. dolor   (ous)   . . . .
4. peril   (ous)   . . . .
5. mountain   (ous)   . . . .
6. beauty   (ous)   . . . .
7. desire   (ous)   . . . .
8. pity   (ous)   . . . .
9. trouble   (ous)   . . . .
10. mischief   (ous)   . . . .
11. plenty   (ous)   . . . .
12. adventure   (ous)   . . . .
13. bounty   (ous)   . . . .
14. danger   (ous)   . . . .
15. grief   (ous)   . . . .
16. humor   (ous)   . . . .
17. outrage   (ous)   . . . .
18. duty   (ous)   . . . .
19. libel   (ous)   . . . .
20. poison   (ous)   . . . .

WORDS ENDING IN *ER* OR *OR*

The suffixes -*er* and -*or* mean *one who* or *that which*. For example, a *visitor* is one who *visits* and an *indicator* is *that which indicates*.

When should you use -*er* and when should you use -*or*?

Although there are many words with these suffixes, unfortuately there is no rule governing their use. The lack of rule, however, need not disturb you. Simply remember that most words end in *-or*. Then study the list of *-er* words below and pay attention to those you use most often.

Twenty-five common words ending in *or*

actor	escalator
administrator	governor
author	indicator
aviator	inventor
bachelor	investigator
collector	operator
commentator	radiator
conductor	refrigerator
contractor	senator
counselor	spectator
editor	sponsor
educator	supervisor
elevator	

Sixteen common words ending in *er*

advertiser	manager
beginner	manufacturer
bookkeeper	passenger
consumer	purchaser
employer	receiver
farmer	stenographer
interpreter	treasurer
laborer	writer

WORDS ENDING IN *AR*

A relatively small number of words end in *-ar*. The most common are listed below. If you study the list, this ending should never cause you trouble.

beggar	dollar
calendar	regular
collar	singular

▶ *NOTICE!*

Distinguish between *hangar*, a shelter for housing airplanes, and *hanger*, one who hangs or that which hangs.

EXERCISE 6

Add the suffix *-or*, *-er*, or *-ar* to each of the following words:

1. begg _ _
2. receiv _ _
3. conduct _ _
4. passeng _ _
5. govern _ _
6. labor _ _
7. operat _ _
8. doll _ _
9. supervis _ _
10. stenograph _ _

TROUBLESOME AFFIXES

The affixes -*al*, *el*, and -*le* are confusing because they are pronounced in approximately the same way.

Although there are no hard-and-fast rules governing their use, here are some guide lines which will help you spell correctly most of the words in which they occur.

THE AFFIX *AL*

The affix -*al* is added to nouns and adjectives only. It means *of*, *belonging to*, *pertaining to*, or *appropriate to*. If you remember these meanings, you will scarcely make a mistake. For example: *personal*, of the person; *autumnal*, belonging to autumn; *royal*, pertaining to a king; *nautical*, appropriate to ships.

Twenty-five common adjectives ending in *al*

additional	magical
adverbial	mechanical
annual	medical
brutal	neutral
classical	normal
clerical	original
comical	oval
fatal	penal
fiscal	personal
general	regal
jovial	several
legal	trivial
logical	

Ten common nouns ending in *al*

acquittal	proposal
arrival	recital
betrayal	refusal
capital	rival
denial	signal

▶ *CAUTION!*

Do not confuse *capital*, a city, with *capitol*, a building.

THE AFFIX *EL*

The affix -*el* originally diminished the meaning of a word to which it was attached. For example, tunnel once meant a small barrel or tun, and chapel meant a small church. Nowadays the original significance of -*el* is forgotten.

If you remember that -*el* is used less frequently than -*al* and if you memorize the spelling of the common words below, you will greatly reduce the possibility of misspelling words in which it appears.

Twenty common words ending in *el*

bushel	kernel
cancel	model
channel	morsel
flannel	novel
funnel	nickel
jewel	panel
kennel	parcel

quarrel	swivel
satchel	travel
shovel	trowel

THE AFFIX *LE*

The affix -*le* is used far more frequently than -*al* or -*el*.

1. Examine the following list carefully.
2. Form a mental image of each word.
3. Pronounce each word aloud. Then write it in the air with your finger. Underline the -*le* after you complete writing the word in the air.
4. Pronounce the word again.

When you perform these steps, you are visualizing, feeling, and hearing. In other words you are employing three senses to help you remember the correct spelling.

able	bundle
ample	bungle
angle	cattle
apostle	chuckle
article	circle
ankle	couple
baffle	cripple
battle	castle
beetle	corpuscle
bottle	dangle
brittle	dazzle
buckle	disciple

double	nibble
dribble	nuzzle
drizzle	paddle
fable	peaceable
fickle	people
fiddle	pestle
frizzle	pickle
gable	possible
gentle	prattle
giggle	principle
girdle	puzzle
gristle	raffle
grizzle	rankle
handle	riddle
huddle	ruffle
humble	scribble
hurdle	scruple
jangle	scuffle
jingle	scuttle
juggle	settle
jungle	shuffle
knuckle	shackle
ladle	shuttle
mantle	sickle
miracle	sizzle
muffle	sparkle
muscle	sprinkle
muzzle	squabble
myrtle	strangle
needle	subtle
nestle	tackle
nettle	thimble

thistle	trifle
treble	triple
tremble	trouble
trestle	turtle
trickle	twinkle

EXERCISE 7

Select the word in each pair which is correctly spelled.

1. a. brutel	b. brutal	. . . . . .
2. a. proposal	b. proposale	. . . . . .
3. a. flannel	b. flannal	. . . . . .
4. a. dangle	b. dangel	. . . . . .
5. a. drizzel	b. drizzle	. . . . . .
6. a. corpuscle	b. corpuscel	. . . . . .
7. a. fatal	b. fatel	. . . . . .
8. a. swivle	b. swivel	. . . . . .
9. a. tripel	b. triple	. . . . . .
10. a. signel	b. signal	. . . . . .
11. a. battle	b. battel	. . . . . .
12. a. quarrle	b. quarrel	. . . . . .
13. a. rankel	b. rankle	. . . . . .
14. a. mechanicle	b. mechanical	. . . . . .
15. a. angal	b. angle	. . . . . .
16. a. rival	b. rivle	. . . . . .
17. a. jewel	b. jewal	. . . . . .
18. a. nickel	b. nickle	. . . . . .
19. a. girdel	b. girdle	. . . . . .
20. a. tragicle	b. tragical	. . . . . .
21. a. thimble	b. thimbel	. . . . . .

22. a. capital   b. capitle   . . . . . .
23. a. knuckel   b. knuckle   . . . . . .
24. a. parcle   b. parcel.   . . . . . .
25. a. regel   b. regal   . . . . . .

How To Distinguish

Between Homonyms

and Other Confusing Pairs of Words

Earlier in this book we pointed out the necessity for listening carefully in order to hear the words being said. Careless listening will give you the wrong concept of the word and thus you take the first step toward misspelling it.

There are many words in English which sound alike but differ in spelling, as *bear* and *bare*, and *ball* and *bawl*. These words are called homonyms.

Homonyms differ in meaning as well as spelling. You must therefore learn their meaning and spelling.

In the following list, most of the homonyms that cause spelling difficulties are listed, defined, and illustrated in sentences. Spelling exercises appear at intervals.

aisle, n. a narrow passage. The bridal couple walked down the *aisle*.

isle, n. an island. Poets sometimes write about the Golden *Isles*.

already, adv. earlier. We had *already* eaten our lunch.

all ready, adj. all are ready. Mother called the chauffeur when we were *all ready*.

altar, n. a tablelike structure used for religious purposes in a church or out of doors. The bridal couple came toward the *altar*.

alter, v. to make a change. Plastic surgeons can *alter* features.

altogether, adv. entirely. I *altogether* disapprove of such behavior in children.

all together, adj. all in one place. The prisoners were placed *all together* in one room.

berth, n. a place to sleep. We ordered a *berth* on the train.

birth, n. act of being born. The *birth* of the prince caused much joy.

born, pp. that which has been given birth. The baby was *born* at dawn.

borne, pp. carried. The countess was *borne* in her sedan chair.

brake, n. an instrument to stop something. Because the *brake* was broken, the car rushed downhill.

break, v. to smash, cause to fall apart. Be careful not to *break* these rare glasses.

bridal, adj. pertaining to a wedding. The *bridal* gown was of taffeta.

bridle, n. part of a harness. The horse pulled at his *bridle*.

bridle, v. to restrain. Some gossips need to *bridle* their tongues.

canvas, n. a kind of rough cloth. The sailor's duffel bag was of *canvas*.

canvass, v. to solicit. Election workers went out to *canvass* the neighborhood.

capital, n. a major city of a state or nation; also, something of extreme importance; also, stock of wealth. Albany is the *capital* of New York. Kidnapping in some states is a *capital* offense. Liberia welcomes foreign *capital*.

capitol, n. a building. In Washington the *capitol* is popular with visitors.

censer, n. a religious article. The acolyte slowly swung the *censer*.

censor, n. one who examines for possible evil. The British *censor* examines the script of every new play.

censor, v. to act as a censor. Authors do not wish anyone to *censor* their books.

chord, n. a pleasant combination of tones. The pianist electrified his audience with his opening *chords*.

cord, n. a rope. Can you get me some *cord* to tie these books?

cord, n. a unit to measure fuel wood. He chopped three *cords* of wood today.

EXERCISE 1

Select the correct word in parenthesis, and underline:

1. This story cannot (alter, altar) the situation.
2. Some experts think that cargo will soon be (born, borne) in submarines.
3. If you put your foot on the (break, brake) you will stop the car.
4. Many sincere people oppose (capital, capitol) punishment.
5. The center (aisle, isle) of the church was very wide.
6. When the search party arrived, the fire had (all ready, already) died out.
7. John soon learned that his answers on the examination were (all right, alright).
8. The town drunk was (altogether, all together) beyond help from any social agency.
9. When the attack was sounded, the marines were (all ready, already).
10. Many families have not had to touch their (capitol, capital) for a long time.

coarse, a. vulgar. Such *coarse* language cannot be permitted.

course, n. a way to be followed. In this emergency, only one *course* was indicated. John took the academic *course* in high school.

complement, n. or v. something that completes another. The fresh *complement* of soldiers saved the day.

compliment, n., v. something said in praise. This was the greatest *compliment* he could have paid. The President *complimented* the commander of the submarine for his good work.

council, n. a deliberative body. The city *council* was called into special session.

counsel, n. advice; also an attorney. My *counsel* in this case is to avoid temperature extremes. The defendant's *counsel* made a stirring plea.

councilor, n. one who is a member of a council. The newly elected *councilor* was given an ovation.

counselor, n. an advisor, usually legal. In America we use the expression *counselor* whereas in Britain it is solicitor or barrister.

core, n. a center of fruit. The *core* of my apple was rotten.

corps, n. a unit of people. General Smith commanded the Second Army *Corps*.

descent, n. a going down. Poe's "*Descent* into a Maelstrom" is still exciting to read.

dissent, n. a disagreement. Justice Holmes' *dissents* were famous.

desert, v. to leave behind. It is a terrible crime to *desert* one's child.

dessert, n. the fruit or ice-cream course at the end of a meal. We had sliced peaches for *dessert*.

dual, adj. double. Dr. Jekyll and Mr. Hyde were the *dual* personalities of one man.

duel, n. combat of two men. Hamilton was killed in the *duel* with Burr.

instance, n. example. The lawyer gave *instance* after *instance* of good behavior.

instants, n. plural, meaning moments. Pain was stopped for several *instants* before the operation was continued.

its, pro. The possessive case of it. The baby played with *its* finger.

it's, abbreviated form of *it is*. *It's* too late to go to any restaurant now.

led, v. the past tense of *lead*. The colonel *led* his men to safety.

lead, n. (lĕd) a metal. Plumbers make use of *lead* frequently.

EXERCISE 2

Select the correct word in parenthesis, and underline.

1. England called its Privy (Council, Counsel) into session.
2. It takes an angle of 40° to (compliment, complement) an angle of 50° to make a right angle.
3. To get out of the swamp, there was only one (course, coarse) to follow.
4. The (desert, dessert) at the end of the banquet was delicious.
5. (It's, its) amazing how much you can get in a library.
6. The legislature passed the bill without any (dissent, descent).
7. After many skirmishes the captain (lead, led) his company to victory.
8. The witness refused to answer any question without advice from his (counsel, council).

9. Eisenhower was (formerly, formally) a general.
10. The judge said that he had a (dual, duel) responsibility

miner, n. one who extracts minerals from the earth. Mark Twain frequently wrote about *miners* in the Old West.

minor, a., n. unimportant; below legal age. This injury to the skin was a *minor* one. Alcoholic beverages may not be sold to *minors*.

peace, n. a state of quiet, freedom from war. The U.N. tries hard to keep the *peace*.

piece, n. a portion. A *piece* of pie costs fifteen cents here.

plain, a., n. as adjective, simple, unadorned. In this small town we live in *plain* houses. As a noun, a flat area of land. Many pioneers perished while crossing this *plain*.

plane, n. an airplane; a tool; a flat surface. The *plane* made a forced landing. To smooth the surface, the carpenter used a new type of *plane*. In high school *plane* geometry usually precedes solid geometry.

principal, a., n. as adjective, main, important. These were the *principal* points in Nixon's speech. As a noun, the head official in a school. A *principal* in a modern high school must be a good administrator.

principle, n. a statement of a rule in conduct or in science or mathematics. Archimedes discovered the *principle* of buoyancy in liquids. A candidate for high office must be a man of *principle*.

stationary, a. fixed, attached. The old-fashioned schoolroom had *stationary* desks and chairs.

stationery, n. paper used in correspondence. Hammerhill is making a new kind of typewriter *stationery*.

there, adv. an adverb of place. He placed the package *there*.

their, pro. a possessive pronoun. The soldiers opened *their* kits.

they're, pro. + verb. contraction of they are. "*They're* here," the colonel shouted.

to, prep. with a verb to make an infinitive. *To* err is human; *to* forgive, divine. Preposition with noun or pronoun. Please take this book *to* him. Deliver this package *to* mother.

too, adv. also, more than enough. Father arrived late for the ceremony *too*. Such bad behavior in class was *too* much for the teacher.

two, numeral, the number 2. He received *two* dollars an hour.

waist, n. middle section of the body; a garment. Every woman admires a narrow *waist*. Her *waist* was made of lace.

waste, v., n. to squander, material which is squandered. To *waste* food is almost a crime when so many starve. Many manufacturers dispose of their industrial *wastes* through incineration.

who's, personal pro. a contraction of who is. "*Who's* there?" she asked.

whose, possessive of *who*. We should like to know *whose* coat this is.

your, possessive of *you*. This is *your* hat.

you're, a contraction of you are. "*You're* elected," the chairman shouted.

EXERCISE 3

Select the correct word in parentheses, and underline.

1. An appendectomy can hardly be considered (minor, miner) surgery.
2. He was a great admirer of (peace, piece) by friendly negotiation.

3. Because of motor difficulties the (plane, plain)
   had to make a forced landing on the (plane,
   plain).
4. The (principle, principal) causes of World
   War II are not easy to state.
5. The young girl placed the belt around her
   (waste, waist).
6. The sailors threw (their, there) caps into the
   air.
7. This insolence was (to, too, two) much to bear.
8. It is not necessary to use expensive (stationery,
   stationary) on minor occasions.
9. We could never discover (whose, who's) book
   it was.
10. "(They're, their) here," exclaimed the teacher.

OTHER CONFUSING PAIRS

There are many other word pairs that are often
confused because they sound almost alike, as *illusion* and *allusion*.
Strictly speaking, such pairs are not homonyms. However, they
cause spelling difficulties and for that reason are listed and defined below. So, too, are words that resemble one another so
closely in spelling that they are a frequent source of trouble, as
moral and *morale*, and *dairy* and *diary*.

advice, n. counsel. We asked the teacher for *advice*.

advise, v. to give counsel. Our parents are ready to *advise* us.

ally, v. to joint with. England can usually be expected to *ally* herself with the United States.

ally, n. one who joins with another. France was our *ally* in World
War II.

lley, n. a narrow thoroughfare. The cat disappeared down the *alley*.

llusion, n. a reference to. The judge made an *allusion* to an old ruling.

lusion, n. a deception. Some people suffer from *illusions*.

ngel, n. a supernatural being. Disputes about *angels* are found in medieval thought.

ngle, n. corner, point of view. Advertisers are always looking for a new *angle*.

eside, prep. by the side of. The bride stood *beside* her husband.

esides, adv. in addition to. *Besides* a bonus, he received a raise.

reath, n. an exhalation. The *breath* froze in the cold air.

reathe, v. to take in or let our breath. The doctor asked the patient to *breathe* in deeply.

loths, n. bits of cloth. Try using new wash *cloths*.

lothes, n. covering for the human body. Beau Brummel's *clothes* were the talk of London.

onsul, n. an official in one country representing another. The Russian *consul* in the United States represents his country's interests.

ounsel, n. an attorney. The *counsel* for the defense entered a plea of guilty.

redible, a. believable. The witness made her story *credible*.

reditable, a. praiseworthy. The soldier's action was *creditable*.

esert, n. dry, barren ground. The Gobi *desert* is vast.

esert, v., n. to abandon. The cowardly soldier tried to *desert*.

evice, n. a contrivance. The inventor showed his new *device* for producing electricity.

devise, v. to make a contrivance. The inventor *devised* a new means of producing electricity.

emigrant, n. one who leaves a country for another. America welcomes *emigrants* of good character from many lands.

immigrant, n. one who comes to another country after leaving his own. Forty million immigrants brought many resources to America.

formally, adv. done in a formal or regular manner. The bridegroom was dressed *formally*.

formerly, adv. earlier. *Formerly*, soldiers had to wait a long time for promotion.

ingenious, a. clever, tricky. The device for operating the ship was *ingenious*.

ingenuous, a. open, frank, innocent. The *ingenuous* countenance of the pretty witness won over the jury.

later, adv. comparative degree of late. It's *later* than you think.

latter, a. of two things, the one mentioned second. Of the two desserts, ice-cream or sherbert, I chose the *latter*.

EXERCISE 4

Select the correct word in parentheses, and underline.

1. He likes to wear brightly colored (clothes, cloths).
2. This development in art comes in a (later, latter) period in history.
3. Refugees in Hong Kong rushed to the American (consul, counsel) for safety.
4. Before signing this contract, you should get legal (advice, advise).

5. He placed the boxes (beside, besides) the wall.
6. During the early part of this century, many (immigrants, emigrants) from England went to Australia.
7. All those who attended the banquet were (formerly, formally) attired.
8. The young child had an (ingenious, ingenuous) countenance.
9. During the last war, the United States was an (ally, alley) of England.
10. The orator's speech was full of literary (illusions, allusions).

loose, a. free, unattached. The screw was *loose*.

lose, v. to miss from one's possession. I would not like to *lose* any more money at the races.

moral, a., n. pertaining to the good and proper. Man lives by *moral* law as well as man-made law.

morale, n. state of well-being of a person or group. The *morale* of our troops in the Middle East was high.

personal, a. pertaining to a person or individual. Our quarrel in the office was not due to a business but to a *personal* argument.

personnel, n. the body of persons employed in some service. Because he had a deep understanding of people, he was appointed *personnel* manager.

quiet, a. free from noise. In hospital areas, *quiet* must be preserved.

quite, a. entirely, completely. The patient was *quite* conscious throughout the operation.

than, cj. a conjunction. Gold is heavier *than* silver.

then, adv. an adverb of time. We shall await you *then*.

EXERCISE 5

Select the correct word in parentheses, and underline.

1. Good food cannot always contribute to high (moral, morale) in the army.
2. Such demands are (quiet, quite) impossible to meet.
3. Problems of (personal, personnel) always arise where there are many employees.
4. The (loose, lose) stone caused the scout to slip.
5. Love is more powerful (then, than) hate.
6. I was (formally, formerly) dressed for the occasion.
7. Where did you (lose, loose) the money?
8. Every fable has a (moral, morale).
9. The tree-shaded street was (quite, quiet) deserted.
10. Rather (than, then) take a risk, he put his money in a bank.

Some Special Difficulties

Because various letters are pronounced alike in English, difficulties in spelling arise. Originally the letter *c* was pronounced as a *k*. We know that, because the old Romans of 2,000 years ago sounded it that way. They had a word *centum,* which means "one hundred." Today, when a student in high school studies Latin, he says *kentum* (like kennel). But this same word in Italian is pronounced *chento* (cento); in French it is *saunt* (cent). Because it came into English from the French back in the days of the Norman conquest of 1066, our word *cent* is really one-hundredth part of something and is pronounced *sent*. This similarity of pronunciation between *c* and *s* is responsible for the confusion in spelling words ending in *-cede, -ceed,* and *-sede*.

SEDE

You should never forget the single word ending in *-sede*. It is *supersede*.

CEED

You can easily remember all the words in *-ceed*. There are only three:

exceed   proceed   succeed

If you want a little device to aid your memory with these words, think of boxer. First, he is a *pro* fessional. When he is past his prime, he is an *ex*-fighter; then he has a *suc* cessor.

CEDE

All the other words in this class end in -cede. Some are:

accede	recede
precede	secede
concede	

EXERCISE 1

Have the following passage read aloud to you as you spell the italicized words. If you misspell any, study the reason for the error. Follow the procedure outlined on page 17 for mastering difficult words until you have learned all the words in this group.

Little countries no longer like to *accede* to the wishes of large countries. In many parts of the world the old type of imperialism has been *superseded*. Wars over natural resources are *receding* into history, to be *succeeded* by pacts of mutual interest. Although we cannot be *excessively* optimistic about hopes for permanent peace, we must *concede* that the outlook is bright. The *successor* to the old-time viceroy is the new representative of the former colonial power who *intercedes* in his country's interest, but is always willing to listen to the other side. Such mutual respect must *precede* any plan for world-wide disarmament and eventual peace.

Better Spelling By Ear

It has been mentioned before that an impression conveyed by several senses will remain longer in the mind than one coming through only one sense organ. Most human beings are visual-minded. They form only an eye-impression of the things they learn. Some people (musicians especially) are ear-minded. You may discover that you are ear-minded by employing the following spelling devices.

Although English has been rightly accused of not being spelled exactly as it sounds, the fact remains that thousands of words *are spelled* precisely as they are pronounced. If you pronounce these words correctly when you are in doubt about them, you will find no difficulty in spelling them.

SPELLING BY PRONUNCIATION

You must first understand something about *syllables* and *syllabication*. The late E. L. Thorndike of Columbia University in his *Century Junior Dictionary* defined a syllable as "part of a word pronounced as a unit consisting of a vowel alone or with one or more consonants."

do	—	word of one syllable
dough nut	—	word of two syllables
syl la ble	—	word of three syllables

▶ *RULES!*

Dividing a Word Into Syllables

1. A consonant between two vowels is pronounced with the later syllable when the first vowel is long.

EXAMPLE:

ro man tic

The consonant *m* begins the second syllable because the vowel *o* is long.
Others: ro tate, Mo hawk, na ture, E den

2. A consonant between two vowels is pronounced with the first vowel if it is short.

The long vowels are pronounced exactly as they are pronounced when you recite the alphabet.

EXAMPLE:

ā — as in hay
ē — as in bee
ī — as in kite
ō — as in note
ū — as in mute

The short vowels are present in this sentence:

That hen is not hungry.

A more amusing instance:

Patter, petter, pitter, potter, putter

Syllables with short vowels:

a — fash ion, tap es try
e — nec es sa ry
i — crit i cism
o — prom i nent
u — sub urb

3. Adjoining consonants most often separate into syllables.

EXAMPLES:

mur mur, can dy, ex pense

4. Double consonants are not divided when a suffix is added.

EXAMPLES:

mill er, hiss ing

These rules should help you also in dividing words at the end of a line. Study the syllabication of the following words that are associated with the automobile:

car bu ret or	man u fac ture
per form ance	pneu mat ic
bat ter y	se dan

It was one of the principles of the government of Ancient Rome to "divide and conquer." The same rule might apply for long words. Divide them into their component syllables and you can conquer them.

SPELLING AS YOU PRONOUNCE
SYLLABLE BY SYLLABLE

Many words appear difficult to spell until we pronounce them carefully. They fall naturally into simple syllables and their difficulty disappears.

▶ *METHOD!*

1. Pronounce the word slowly.
2. Spell it aloud *by syllables.*
3. Pronounce it slowly twice more, writing as you do so.

4. Pronounce it quickly in a sentence, writing the whole sentence.

Each of the words following loses all its terror when thus approached.

ac com mo date	en deav or
ac know ledge	priv i lege
mag nif i cent	dis ap pear
Wed nes day	dis ar range
mag a zine	in ter pre ted

In this section are lists of words that have had their thousands of victims. Have someone dictate these words to you. Spell them. Then compare your spelling with those in the book. The ones you have spelled correctly, you need no longer bother with. Your misspelled words, you must examine. What errors did you make? There is an entire section for each error. Practice the words until you can spell them correctly without the need of thinking twice about them. These words may all be learned by accustoming your ear to hear them correctly.

Each of the following words has *a* trouble. People forget the existence of *a* and substitute another letter:

captain	certain	calendar
finally	grammar	illegal
		criminal
maintain	plain	dictionary
preparations	probable	liberal
separate	straight	justifiable
usually	villain	
balance	equivalent	
performance	salary	
actually	extravagant	equally
village	capital	congressional

partially	principal	professional
radical	similar	temperature

Each of the words below has an *e* difficulty. Writers frequently forget the *e* and use another letter incorrectly.

apparently	competent	conscience
dependent	coherent	audience
prominent	current	correspondence
machinery	efficient	existence
independent	experience	magnificent
stationery	opponent	patience
privileges	permanent	superintendent
luncheon	cafeteria	description

In the following words, the *i*'s have it:

acquainted	auxiliary	business
compliment	definite	exhibition
criticized	sympathized	until
participle	peculiar	principle
quantities	quiet	respectively
physical	individual	hosiery
articles	rime	anticipate

Omitting the *o*'s. In the words below, the letter *o* comes in for much abuse and neglect. Be kind to these words:

attorney	authorize	competitors
conspicuous	conqueror	editor
favorable	memorial	minor
notorious	organization	senator
society	strenuously	tailor

Supplementary exercises:

odor	aviator	capitol
colonel	accustomed	authority
colors	favorite	interior
humorist	memory	motorist
precious	proprietor	successor
surgeon		

Concentrate on the double letters in these words. They are the cause of many common errors:

accommodate	agreed	agreeable
beginning	committee	guaranteed
embarrass	loose	proceed
necessary	parallel	succeed
recommend	speech	too
across	baggage	assistance
dissatisfaction	affirmative	appearance
disappeared	chauffeur	appropriate
disappointed		disapproved
illegible	immigrant	interrupted
occasion		Mediterranean
opposite	possession	professor

It used to be said of children that they should be seen and not heard. These words have letters that are often not seen when writing. Don't omit them:

government	promptly	February
indebted	pamphlet	pledged
	condemn	

REVERSALS

A common type of misspelling occurs when letters are interchanged. For example, *l* and *v* are often reversed in *relevant* so that the word is misspelled *revelant*.

This type of error is called *metathesis*.

Observe the correct spelling of the following ten words:

Correct	*Incorrect*
cava*l*ry	ca*l*vary
child*ren*	child*ern*
hund*red*	hund*erd*
jewe*l*ry	jew*l*ery
lar*ynx*	lar*nyx*
mod*ern*	mod*ren*
patt*ern*	patt*ren*
*per*spiration	*pre*spiration
re*lev*ant	re*vel*ant
west*ern*	west*ren*

▶ *NOTICE!*

The mountain mentioned in the Bible is Calvary. It is spelled with a capital C and should not be confused with cavalry, a troop of horsemen.

EXERCISE 1

Fill in the missing letters:

1. hund _ _ d
2. mod _ _ n
3. p _ _ spiration
4. west _ _ n
5. re _ e _ ant
6. ca _ a _ ry
7. child _ _ n
8. jew _ _ _ y
9. lar _ _ x
10. patt _ _ n

Help for Spanish-Speaking Students

Spanish words are easy to spell because almost every letter represents only one sound and every letter is pronounced.

Spanish speakers find some English words difficult to spell because some letters represent more than one sound and some letters are not pronounced.

Spanish spelling is logical and predictable. English spelling is inconsistent and not always controlled by rules.

If your native language is Spanish, the following hints will help you spell English words correctly.

DIFFERENT SPELLINGS FOR THE SAME SOUND

There are some sounds which are the same in Spanish and English yet differ in spelling.

For example, Spanish words with an *f* sound are sometimes spelled with a *ph* in English. The sound is the same but the spelling is different.

Examine the spelling of the following words:

catástrofe   catastro*ph*e

farmacéutico	*ph*armacist
farmacia	*ph*armacy
frase	*ph*rase
filósofo	*ph*ilosopher
fotografía	*ph*otogra*ph*
geografía	geogra*ph*y
hemisferio	hemis*ph*ere
párrafo	paragra*ph*
teléfono	tele*ph*one
triunfante	trium*ph*ant

▶ *NOTICE!*

All the words in the above list are derived from Greek. In such words the sound of *f* is spelled *ph* in English. In most other English words *f* is used; for example, *f*riend, pre*f*er, scar*f*.

The sound represented by *cu* in Spanish is spelled *qu* in English, as you may see from the following words:

cuestión	*qu*estion
frecuente	fre*qu*ent
frecuentemente	fre*qu*ently

The vowel in s*i*, qu*i*, am*i*go is also an English sound. In Spanish this sound is represented by *i*. In English there are ten different ways of representing this sound as shown below.

ae	*Ae*sop, C*ae*sar
ay	qu*ay*
e	*e*ternal, sc*e*nic, conv*e*ne
ea	*ea*ch, b*ea*n, t*ea*
ee	*ee*ry, sl*ee*k

ei	*ei*ther, inv*ei*gle, rece*i*ve
eo	p*eo*ple
ey	k*ey*
i	mach*i*ne, rav*i*ne, fat*i*gue, cl*i*que
ie	pr*ie*st, ser*ie*s

EXERCISE 1

Indicate at the right whether the following English words are correctly spelled. Place a C if correct and an X if wrong. If a word is misspelled, spell it correctly.

1. farmacy ......
2. photograf ......
3. philosopher ......
4. geography ......
5. frecuently ......
6. eather ......
7. machene ......
8. triumfant ......
9. peeple ......
10. priest ......
11. recieve ......
12. paragraf ......
13. sereis ......
14. convean ......
15. fatiegue ......

In Spanish the letter *u* (puro, Cuba) represents a sound which is also used in English but spelled differently. Note that there are several ways of spelling this sound:

oo	g*oo*se, al*oo*f, sp*oo*n, r*oo*ster, t*oo*
ou	gr*ou*p, tr*ou*pe, ac*ou*stic, b*ou*quet
ough	thr*ough*

u	r*u*ler, br*u*tal
ui	fr*ui*t, s*ui*table
o	d*o*, t*o*, tw*o*

▶ *NOTICE!*

The confusion of *to*, *too*, and *two* is a common error. Be sure you know the difference.

to	a preposition meaning the opposite of *from*; the sign of the infinitive.
EXAMPLES:	
	to the theatre, to go
two	an adjective meaning twice one.
EXAMPLE:	
	two friends
too	an adverb meaning also or more than enough.
EXAMPLE:	
	too late

Here is a sentence in which the three words are used correctly: The two friends wanted to go to the theatre but they were too late.

EXERCISE 2

Every word below is misspelled. Cross it out and spell it correctly.

1. truip ....
2. brootal ....
3. sootable ....
4. ruster ....
5. throo ....

6. acoostic　　　. . . . .
7. aluf　　　　　. . . . .
8. ruiler　　　　. . . . .
9. booquet　　　. . . . .
10. guis　　　　　. . . . .

EXERCISE 3

Compose a sentence in which *to*, *too*, and *two* are used correctly.

DOUBLE CONSONANTS

There are only two double consonants in Spanish, *ll* and *rr*. There are many in English.

Observe that the English words listed below have double consonants while their Spanish counterparts have only one.

cc	el acento	accent
	el acuerdo	accord
	el oculto	occult
	ocupado	occupied
	ocurrir	occur
	aceptar	accept
ff	diferente	different
	sufrir	suffer
	suficiente	sufficient
gg	exagerado	exaggerated
ll	la alianza	alliance
	el dólar	dollar
	inteligente	intelligent
mm	común	common
	gramática	grammar

pp	aparecer	a*pp*ear
	apetito	a*pp*etite
	aplaudir	a*pp*laud
	aprender	a*pp*rehend
	aproximadamente	a*pp*roximately
tt	ataque	a*tt*ack
	atención	a*tt*ention
	batalla	ba*tt*le
	botella	bo*tt*le
	botón	bu*tt*on

EXERCISE 4

Some of the following words are spelled correctly and some are misspelled. Put a check in the blank if a word is spelled correctly. Re-write it correctly if it is misspelled.

1. acord ....
2. dollar ....
3. ocurr ....
4. appetite ....
5. aprehend ....
6. aproximately ....
7. applaud ....
8. sufer ....
9. buton ....
10. aliance ....
11. accept ....
12. ocupied ....
13. diferent ....
14. gramar ....
15. exaggerated ....
16. apear ....
17. suficient ....

18. atention . . . .
19. battle . . . .
20. occult . . . .

▶ *NOTICE!*

Double consonants are more common in English than in Spanish. Consult the rules on pages 29-37 for doubling consonants. You will find them helpful.

WORDS WITH *J*

In Spanish, *j* is pronounced like English *h* in *hello!*, *have*, and *here*. The English *j* sound does not exist in Spanish. It resembles Spanish *ch* in *muchacho* except that it is voiced.

To understand the meaning of a voiced consonant, put your fingers on each side of your voice box (larynx). Say the sounds of *m*, *n*, *r*. Can you feel your vocal cords vibrate? These are called voiced consonants because they are made with the aid of the vocal cords.

Now say the sound of *ch*. Notice that your vocal cords do not vibrate. A consonant made without vibration of the vocal cords is called a voiceless consonant.

The English *j* sound is spelled in different ways:

di	cor*di*al, sol*di*er
dg	bri*dg*e, fu*dg*e, slu*dg*e
g	*g*em, *g*ist, alle*g*e, ma*g*ic, lon*g*itude, lon*g*evity, an*g*el, dan*g*er
gg	su*gg*est
j	*j*ade, *j*ar, *J*apan, *j*ail, *j*eer, *j*ealousy, *j*elly, *j*ingle, *j*ockey, *j*ostle, *j*udge, *j*ury

EXERCISE 5

Each of the following words contains the sound

of *j*. Insert the missing letter or letters.

1. alle_e
2. lon_evity
3. an_el
4. _ostle
5. _ealousy
6. su _ _ est
7. cor _ _ al
8. sol _ _ er
9. _ist
10. _eer

SILENT LETTERS

In many English words there are silent letters. They are written but not pronounced.

Silent d	We*d*nesday
Silent g	*g*narled, *g*nash, *g*nat, forei*g*n, rei*g*n, sovarei*g*n
Silent h	*h*eir, *h*erb, *h*onor, *h*our, shep*h*erd, fore*h*ead
Silent k	*k*nee, *k*night, *k*nock, *k*now, *k*nowledge
Silent l	a*l*mond, a*l*ms, ca*l*f, ca*l*m, cha*l*k, fo*l*k, ha*l*f, Linco*l*n, psa*l*m, so*l*dier, ta*l*k, wa*l*k, yo*l*k
Silent n	condem*n*, dam*n*, hym*n*, solem*n*
Silent p	cor*p*s, cu*p*board, *p*neumonia, *p*sychology, *p*tomaine, ras*p*berry
Silent t	chas*t*en, fas*t*en, glis*t*en, has*t*en, lis*t*en, mois*t*en, of*t*en, sof*t*en, epis*t*le, hus*t*le, jos*t*le, nes*t*le, this*t*le

EXERCISE 6
Replace the silent letter in each of these words:

1. _night
2. _salm
3. epis_le
4. cor_s
5. sof_en
6. We_nesday
7. _naw
8. fas_en
9. rei_n
10. lis_en
11. hym_
12. ras_berry
13. _onor
14. cu_board
15. mois_en

THE *OUGH* COMBINATION

The -ough combination causes everyone difficulty. There are no rules governing the spelling of words containing it. You must memorize each word individually.

Carefully examine the following words and memorize their spelling:

Word	*-ough pronounced as in:*
although, thorough, thoroughfare	*go*
through, throughout, slough (a swamp)	*you*
bought, ought, sought	*saw*
tough, slough (to shed or cast off)	*cuff*
cough	*awful*
hiccough	*up*
drought	*cow*

EXERCISE 7
Fill in each blank with a word selected from the list above.

1. He continued to work .... he wasn't feeling well.
2. The .... ran .... the center of the city.
3. The purchaser .... some .... medicine in the drugstore.
4. People who are very ill .... to see a doctor.
5. Hemp is a .... fiber.
6. A long severe .... ruined the crops .... the countryside.
7. Some snakes .... off their skins annually.
8. A .... may be embarrassing.

THE *IGH* AND *EIGH* COMBINATIONS

The -*igh* and -*eigh* combinations look frightening but they are really very simple and you can master the spelling of words in which they appear within a few minutes.

The combination -*igh* is always pronounced like the diphthong in Spanish h*ay* and fr*ai*le.

Native Spanish speakers tend to spell *might*, *sight*, and similar words as *mait* and *sait* in accordance with the Spanish pattern. If you carefully study the following list, which contains the most common -igh words, you will not make this mistake.

blight	night
bright	playwright
fight	sight
flight	slight
fright	tight

frighten   tighten
might

The combination *-eigh* is pronounced like the diphthong in r*ei*na and l*ey*. There are only two exceptions to this rule, *height* and *sleight*, which are pronounced as if they were spelled *jait* and *slait* in Spanish.

▶ *NOTICE!*

Usually *i* precedes *e* in English (e.g. *grieve, piece*). However, in *-eigh*, *e* precedes *i*.

Examine the following list:

eight   sleigh
freight   weigh
neigh   weight
neighbor

EXERCISE 8

Fill the blanks with *igh* or *eigh*:

1. fr . . . . . t
2. w . . . . . t
3. m . . . . . t
4. n . . . . . bor
5. sl . . . . . t
6. t . . . . . t
7. n . . . . . t
8. fr . . . . . t
9. playwr . . . . . t
10. s . . . . . t

THE *TION* ENDING

Words which end with *ción* in Spanish (for example, *habitación*) are spelled with *tion* in English.

The ending *ción* does not occur in English. Examine the list below:

admiración   admiration
atención   attention

atracción	attraction
construcción	construction
distinción	distinction
excepción	exception
irritación	irritation
preposición	preposition
producción	production
pronunciación	pronunciation
tentación	te*mp*tation
tradición	tradition

WORDS BEGINNING WITH *SP* AND *ST*

Examine these pairs of words:

especial	special
espacio	space
espectáculo	spectacle
espíritu	spirit
establo	stable
estación	station
estado	state
estatua	statue
estilo	style
estómago	stomach
estudio	study
estudiante	student

Have you noticed that Spanish words beginning with *esp* and *est* drop the initial *e* when they become English? If you are aware of this, you will avoid a common spelling error.

EXERCISE 9

Write the English equivalent of each of the following:

1. espectaculo . . . .
2. atención . . . .
3. estatua . . . .
4. construcción . . . .
5. estudio . . . .
6. pronunciación . . . .
7. espacio . . . .
8. tradición . . . .
9. estómago . . . .
10. producción . . . .

Spelling Abbreviations

DAYS OF THE WEEK

Sun.	Sunday
Mon.	Monday
Tues.	Tuesday
Wed.	Wednesday
Thurs.	Thursday
Fri.	Friday
Sat.	Saturday

MONTHS OF THE YEAR

Jan.	January
Feb.	February
Mar.	March
Apr.	April
Aug.	August
Sept.	September
Oct.	October
Nov.	November
Dec.	December

TITLES

Mr.	Mister
Mrs.	Mistress
Messrs.	Messieurs
Dr.	Doctor
D.D.S.	Doctor of Dental Surgery
M.D.	Doctor of Medicine
Ph.D.	Doctor of Philosophy
Gov.	Governor
Pres.	President
Com.	commander commissioner commission committee
Lt.	Lieutenant
Capt.	Captain
Hon.	Honorable
Prof.	Professor
Rev.	Reverend
Supt.	Superintendent
Sec.	Secretary
Treas.	Treasurer
Asst.	Assistant
R.N.	Registered Nurse

DATES

A.D.	anno Domini (Latin for "In the year of the Lord")
B.C.	before Christ
A.M.	ante meridiem (Latin for "before noon")
P.M.	post meridiem (Latin for "after noon")
E.S.T.	Eastern Standard Time

MEASUREMENT

in.	inch	bu.	bushel
ft.	foot	doz.	dozen
yd.	yard	hr.	hour
oz.	ounce	yr.	year
lb.	pound		

BUSINESS

Assn.	Association	St.	Street
acct.	account	Ave.	Avenue
ad	advertisement	Bldg.	Building
ans.	answer	Blvd.	Boulevard
Inc.	Incorporated	Jr.	Junior
Ltd.	Limited	Sr.	Senior
etc.	and so forth	Esq.	Esquire
no.	number	ult.	last month
dept.	department	recd.	received
Bros.	Brothers	mfg.	manufacturing

CAPITALIZATIONS

P.O.	Post Office
P.S.	Postscript (written after the letter)
R.R.	Railroad
SS	Steamship
Mts.	Mountains
C.O.D.	Collect on Delivery
F.O.B.	Freight on Board
R.F.D.	Rural Free Delivery
R.S.V.P.	Reply if you please (French: répondez s'il vous plaît.)

EXERCISE 1

In the space to the right, put the correct spelling of the abbreviations of the following words:

1. Secretary ....
2. Treasurer ....
3. Collect on Delivery ....
4. Before noon ....
5. Junior ....
6. dozen ....
7. August ....
8. Doctor of Medicine ....
9. Honorable ....
10. year ....
11. Saturday ....
12. Rural Free Delivery ....
13. Reply if you please ....
14. Esquire ....
15. Department ....
16. pound ....
17. Messieurs ....
18. Dentist ....
19. Reverend ....
20. Boulevard ....

EXERCISE 2

Write the words for which the following abbreviations are given:

1. Ph.D. ....
2. Ave. ....
3. in. ....
4. etc. ....
5. no. ....
6. Bros. ....

7. **P.S.** ....
8. **R.R.** ....
9. Sept. ....
10. F.O.B. ....
11. Prof. ....
12. Asst. ....
13. E.S.T. ....
14. Gov. ....
15. B.C. ....
16. A.D. ....
17. SS ....
18. St. ....
19. recd. ....
20. dept. ....
21. M.D. ....
22. Treas. ....
23. Sat. ....
24. Hon. ....
25. Rev. ....
26. Sec. ....
27. D.D.S. ....
28. Capt. ....
29. Mar. ....
30. **P.M.** ....

Space Age Words

Several hundred new words have entered our language to describe space age technology. Some are so recent that they have not yet been included in dictionaries although they frequently appear in newspapers and are part of our daily conversation.

You should know the spelling and meaning of the most common space age words. They are listed below and their spelling difficulties indicated when necessary.

SPACE TERMS

Term	Definition
abort	To terminate; to cut short
aCCeleration	Rate of change of speed
AEROdynamics	Science dealing with force of air in motion (Note: a singular noun)
air-to-air missILE	A missile launched in the air against an air-borne target (Use hyphens because the two nouns form an adjective)

air-to-surface missILE	A missile launched in the air against a target on land or sea
antimissILE missILE	A missile designed to destroy other missiles in flight
antisatellite missILE	A missile designed to destroy a satellite in flight
ballistic missILE	A missile which follows a ballistic trajectory after the force of its initial thrust is ended
guided missILE	A missile whose flight path can be changed by a mechanism within it
apogEE	The point of an orbit which is at the greatest distance from the earth
asterOIDS	The numerous small planets whose orbits lie between Mars and Jupiter
astronAUT	A space flier
booster	An auxiliary rocket
capsule	A sealed cabin in which humans can live during space flight; it contains mechanisms for the return of its occupants to earth
control rocket	A rocket used to guide a space vehicle

cosmonAUT	A space flier; an astronaut
cosMIC rays	Space radiations
countdown	The timed events preceding a launching expressed in minus quantities (T minus 5, etc.) After launching, plus time is used (T plus 5, etc.)
crater	A depression formed by the impact of a meteor.
digital computer	A computer which solves problems by mathematical processes
drone	An unmanned aircraft remotely controlled
eLLiptical	Pertaining to an ellipse
gaLaxy	A massive collection of stars
gamma ray	A form of electromagnetic radiation
gantry	A structure resembling a crane used to assemble and service large rockets
hypersoNic	Relating to speed faster than sound
inclination	The angle formed by two lines or planes
interstellAR	Relating to space between stars
ion	An atom minus an outer electron

jet propuLsion	A form of propulsion in which the propulsion unit obtains oxygen from the air (In rocket propulsion the unit carries its own oxygen-producing material)
landing rocket	A rocket used to convey passengers from a spacecraft to the moon or earth
light-year	The distance traveled by light in a year (Note the hyphen)
Loran	A long-range electrical navigation system (Note capitalization)
lunar	Relating to the moon
mare	A lunar sea
propeLLant	Liquid or solid fuel burned in rocket engines to provide thrust
MacH number	A number expressing the relationship between the speed of a body and the speed of sound (Notice that Mach is capitalized)
liftoff	The rising of a space vehicle from its launcher (Note that liftoff is not hyphenated)
microwave	A very short radio wavelength (Note that microwave is not hyphenated)

nuCLEAR rocket	A rocket propelled by nuclear fission
pad	A launch pad; a base for a launcher
payload	The equipment or cargo carried on a space mission (Not hyphenated)
periGEE	The point of an orbit which is closest to the earth
piCKaback	Carried as one might carry a person on his shoulders or back
probe	An unmanned space vehicle used for purposes of exploration
quasars	Recently discovered radioactive objects billions of light years from the earth
radAR	A device which emits radio energy and receives reflections of that energy from objects
re-entry	The return of a space vehicle to the earth's atmosphere (Note hyphenation)
roger	A word signifying O.K.
sateLLite	An unpowered space vehicle in orbit around the moon or a planet
scrub	To cancel a launch

soft landing	A landing on the moon or on a planet without a crash
soNic boom	The roar caused by an aircraft flying at speed faster than sound
telEMetry	The radio connection between a missile and a ground station
teRRestial	Relating to the earth
traJectory	A space vehicle's path through space
troPOsphere	The lower layer of the earth's atmosphere

SPACE VEHICLES

Since 1957, when the Soviet Union opened the space age by launching Sputnik I, there have been many space projects and vehicles. They are listed below in alphabetical order for easy reference.

▶ *NOTICE!*

All the names are capitalized. The italicized letters indicate spelling difficulties.

Able	Greb	Samos
Agena	Hitch-hiker	Saturn
A*lou*ette	(Observe	Score
Anna	the hyphen)	Scout
A*pollo*	In*j*un	Sputni*k*
Ariel	Lofti	Star*ad*
Atlas	Luni*k*	Su*r*cal

Beacon	Mariner	Syncom
Centaur	Mars	Telstar
Composite	Midas	Thor
Cosmos	Oscar	Tiros
Courier	Pioneer	Titan
Delta	Polyot	Traac
Discoverer	Radose	Transit
Echo	Ranger	Vanguard
Elektron	Redstone	Venus Probe
Explorer	Relay	Vostok

SPACE ABBREVIATIONS

AC	Alternating current
BMEWS	Ballistics Missiles Early Warning System
G or g	Earth's gravity
ICBM	Intercontinental Ballistics Missile
DOVAP	Doppler Velocity and Positions
LOX	Liquid oxygen
NASA	National Aeronautics and Space Administration
UHF	Ultra high frequency
VHF	Very high frequency
X	Experimental
Y	Prototype (a model used for operational tests)

EXERCISE 1

From each group select the correctly spelled word and place the letter before it in the space at the left.

1. .... a. Apollo b. Appollo c. Apolo
d. Appolo

2. .... a. nuculear, b. nuclaer c. nuclear d. nucclear
3. .... a. trajectory b. tragectory c. tradgectory d. trajerectory
4. .... a. Sputnick b. Sputtnick c. Sputtnik d. Sputnik
5. .... a. asteroyds b. astaroids c. astiroids d. asteroids
6. .... a. hypersonnic b. hypersonic c. hyppersonic d. hyperssonic
7. .... a. tropposphere b. troposphere c. tropospheer d. troposphear
8. .... a. astronnaut b. astronaut c. asternaut d. astornaut
9. .... a. lasser b. lacer c. laser d. laiser
10. .... a. acceleration b. aceleration c. accelleration d. acelleration
11. .... a. Marriner b. Mariner c. Marinar d. Marinner
12. .... a. apogge b. apoggee c. appoge d. apogee
13. .... a. rador b. rader c. radar d. raydor
14. .... a. interrstellar b. intersteller c. intersteler d. interstellar
15. .... a. missile b. missil c. misile d. misle

Exercises In Word-Building

Almost every one of us at least once in his life has wanted to strangle his neighbor's daughter for playing her scale exercises on the piano. The monotony of the same arrangement of notes hour after hour is almost beyond human endurance. Without these scales, however, no virtuoso would ever develop. Spelling, too, has its scales and exercises. They may seem just as boring as the musical exercises, but they are similarly valuable.

Study the following word families. Sometimes you will forget the spelling of one of these words. If you can remember its brother or sister, you will not have to consult the dictionary. A little time spent with these now will mean much time saved later.

WORD FAMILIES

abolish	abolished	abolishing	abolition
accomplish	accomplished	accomplishing	accomplishment
account	accounted	accounting	accountant
acknowledge	acknowledged	acknowledging	acknowledgment
advise	advised	advising	adviser (or advisor)
allude	alluded	alluding	allusion
almost	always	already	altogether
appear	appeared	appearing	appearance

arrange	arranged	arranging	arrangement
arrive	arrived	arriving	arrival
assist	assisted	assisting	assistance
begin	began	beginning	beginner
believe	believed	believing	believer
busy	busied	busying	business
change	changed	changing	changeable
choose	chose	choosing	chosen
complete	completed	completely	completion
confide	confident	confidence	confidentially
conscience	conscientious	subconscious	unconscious
consider	considered	considerable	consideration
continue	continued	continuation	continually
control	controlling	controller	controllable
critic	critical	criticize	criticism
deceive	deceit	deception	deceiver
decide	decided	decision	deciding
define	definite	definition	definitely
describe	descriptive	describing	description
desire	desirous	desiring	desirable
embarrass	embarrassed	embarrassing	embarrassment
endure	endured	endurable	endurance
equip	equipped	equipping	equipment
every	everybody	everywhere	everyone
exceed	exceeded	exceeding	exceedingly
excel	excelled	excellent	excellence
excite	exciting	excitement	excitable
exist	existed	existing	existence
experience	experienced	experiencing	experiment
extend	extended	extensive	extension
impress	impressed	impressive	impression
intend	intended	intensive	intension

interfere	interfered	interfering	interference
interrupt	interrupted	interrupting	interruption
obey	obedient	obedience	obeisance
occasion	occasioned	occasional	occasionally
peace	peaceful	peaceable	peaceably
permit	permitted	permissible	permission
persist	persisted	persistent	persistence
pity	pitied	pitying	pitiable
possess	possessed	possessive	possession
practice	practical	practiced	practicable
prefer	preferred	preferring	preference
recognize	recognized	recognition	recognizable
separate	separation	inseparable	separately
sincere	sincerity	insincere	sincerely
surprise	surprised	surprisingly	surprising

EXERCISE 1

Indicate by the letter C if the following words are correctly spelled. Correct all errors in the space to the right.

1. arranger . . . .
2. choosers . . . .
3. difinative . . . .
4. preferential . . . .
5. inseparable . . . .
6. hypocritical . . . .
7. undefineable . . . .
8. undesireable . . . .
9. pityless . . . .
10. unaccountable . . . .
11. unchangeable . . . .
12. incompletely . . . .
13. disarrange . . . .

14. confiding . . . .
15. confidential . . . .
16. indecisive . . . .
17. non-existant . . . .
18. preferrable . . . .
19. experiential . . . .
20. unendureable . . . .
21. necessarly . . . .
22. transferred . . . .
23. cancel . . . .
24. changable . . . .
25. judgement . . . .
26. accomadate . . . .
27. gaurantee . . . .
28. reciepts . . . .
29. secretary . . . .
30. business . . . .
31. choosen . . . .
32. posessed . . . .
33. reconized . . . .
34. sincereity . . . .
35. existance . . . .
36. embarassed . . . .
37. excellent . . . .
38. exciteable . . . .
39. prefered . . . .
40. ocassion . . . .

Words Most Frequently Misspelled

THE ONE HUNDRED PESTS

ache	could	here	read
again	country	hoarse	ready
always	dear	hour	said
among	doctor	instead	says
answer	does	just	seems
any	done	knew	separate
been	don't	know	shoes
beginning	early	laid	since
believe	easy	lose	some
blue	enough	loose	straight
break	every	making	sugar
built	February	many	sure
business	forty	meant	tear
busy	friend	minute	their
buy	grammar	much	there
can't	guess	none	they
choose	half	often	though
color	having	once	through
coming	hear	piece	tired
cough	heard	raise	tonight

too	used	where	won't
trouble	very	whether	would
truly	wear	which	write
Tuesday	Wednesday	whole	writing
two	week	women	wrote

ATTENTION SECRETARIES AND OTHER OFFICE WORKERS!

The 500 words which follow are those which are most commonly misspelled in business correspondence. If you want to improve your secretarial effectiveness, study these words closely until you can spell every one correctly.

The list was compiled by the National Office Management Association after a comprehensive study of 10,652 letters collected from business concerns and government agencies located throughout the country.

The words are not strange or unusual. They appear frequently in business letters. Many of them appear on other pages of this book. Mastery of this list will insure you against the spelling mistakes committed by many secretaries.

accept	address	aggravate	anticipating
accommodate	adjustable	allotment	anxiety
accountant	administration	allowance	apology
accumulate	advances	all right	apparatus
acknowledgment	advertisement	alphabetic	appearance
acquainted	advisability	aluminum	applicant
acquire	advise	analysis	appraisal
acquisition	affects	analyze	appropriation
acquitted	affidavit	anniversary	approval
actually	affirmative	announcement	argument
additionally	agency	anthracite	arrears

arrival	bulletin	compel	curiosity
articles	bureau	compensation	currency
assessable	business	competent	customer
assignment		complaint	
assistance	calculator	complimentary	decision
associate	calendar	concession	defendant
assured	campaign	condemn	deferred
attached	canceled	conference	deficit
attorney	candidate	confirmation	definite
attempt	capacity	congestion	defray
attendance	capitalization	conscientious	demonstration
attractive	carbon	consequence	depreciation
auditor	carrier	considerable	description
available	cartage	consignee	desperate
aviation	carton	consolidated	destination
	certificate	construction	deteriorate
baggage	chattel	consumer	determination
balance	circular	container	develop
bankruptcy	clearance	contemplating	dictionary
banquet	coincidence	contemporary	director
barrel	collapsible	contingent	disappear
barter	collateral	convenience	disappoint
becoming	collision	conveyance	disastrous
beneficiary	column	cooperate	disbursements
benefited	combination	corporation	discernible
biased	combustible	corroborate	discontinued
bituminous	commerce	corrugated	discrepancy
bookkeeping	commission	counterfeit	discuss
borrower	committee	coupon	dispatch
brief	commodity	courteous	dissatisfaction
broadcast	community	credentials	dissolution
brokerage	companies	creditor	distinction
budget	comparative	cylinder	distinguish

distributor	exhibition	immediately	itinerary
dividend	existence	impracticable	its
document	expedite	inasmuch	
doubt	explanation	inconsistent	jobber
duplicate	extension	inconvenience	journal
durable		incorporated	keenness
	facilitate	incredible	knowledge
earliest	February	increment	
earnest	financier	indelible	laboratory
easier	foreclosure	indemnity	ladies
economic	forehead	indispensable	latter
eighth	forfeit	inducement	leased
elevator	formally	industrial	ledger
eligible	formerly	inevitable	legitimate
embarrass	forty	inferred	leisure
emergency	franchise	inflation	liabilities
enormous	fundamental	infringement	library
enterprise	furniture	initiate	license
envelope	futile	inquiry	likable
equally		insolvency	liquidation
equipped	generally	inspection	literature
especially	genuine	instance	lucrative
estimate	government	institution	luscious
essentially	grammar	instructor	luxury
eventually	handkerchief	insurance	
evidence	hastily	integrity	machinery
exaggerate	hazard	intelligence	maintenance
examination	height	interpretation	management
exasperate	hoping	inventory	manila
excellent	hosiery	investigate	manufacturer
except	humorous	invoice	margin
exchange		involved	material
executive	illegible	itemized	maturity

mechanical	oneself	photostat	readjustment
medicine	opportunity	physical	really
memorandum	optimism	physician	reasonable
merchandise	option	plaintiff	rebate
mercantile	ordinance	plausible	receipt
merge	organization	policy	recognize
middleman	outrageous	practically	recommend
mimeograph	overdraw	precedence	reconstruction
miniature	overhead	precise	reference
miscellaneous	oxygen	preface	regardless
misrepresent		preference	register
misspelled	pamphlet	prescription	reimburse
moistener	parallel	presence	reinforcement
monopoly	parenthesis	presidency	relations
mortgage	parliament	prestige	remedied
movie	particularly	primitive	remittance
mucilage	pavilion	principal	representative
municipal	peaceable	principle	requisition
	peculiarities	privilege	resign
necessary	pecuniary	procedure	respectfully
ninth	per cent	process	respectively
notary	perforation	professional	responsible
noticeable	performance	prominence	restaurant
notwithstanding	permanent	promissory	ridiculous
nowadays	permissible	pronunciation	rural
	perpendicular	prospectus	
obliging	perseverance	psychology	sacrifice
observation	personal		salary
obsolete	personnel	qualification	salutation
obstacle	persuade	quantity	sanitary
occasionally	perusal	questionnaire	satisfactory
occurred	petition	quotation	schedule
omission	petroleum		scissors

secretarial	speculate	susceptible	unanimous
security	statement	syllable	university
seize	stationary	syndicate	unmistakable
separate	stationery	systematize	utilities
several	statistics		utilize
significance	straightened	tangible	
similar	strenuous	tariff	verification
simultaneous	strictly	tendency	visible
sincerely	sublet	testimonials	vicinity
sociable	subsidize	tickler	volume
society	substantial	together	voucher
solemn	substitute	transferred	
solvent	subtle	transparent	waive
sometimes	successful	treasurer	warrant
source	suggestion	triplicate	Wednesday
southern	summary	Tuesday	whatever
souvenir	superfluous	turnover	wholesale
specialize	superintendent	typewriter	wholly
specify	surplus	typographical	women
spectacular	surprise	typical	

TEST YOURSELF ON A NATIONAL EXAMINATION

The following words are among those office workers and students frequently misspell. You may notice that some of them have been discussed in previous pages of this book. You should profit from this repetition.

First, study the list carefully. Next, ask a friend to dictate the words to you and write them as he dictates them. Have him check off the words you misspelled. Study these words. Have your friend dictate these words to you. You can repeat this process until you have mastered all the words.

1. equation
2. bankruptcy
3. partially
4. effect (result)
5. likable
6. reward
7. advantageous
8. nominal
9. certificate
10. campaign
11. obsolete
12. earnest
13. excessive
14. triumph
15. youthfulness
16. atomic
17. manufacturer
18. jewelry
19. advertisement
20. believe
21. existence
22. deductible
23. benevolent
24. eighth
25. grammar
26. bargain
27. visible
28. offered
29. absence
30. deceive
31. decision
32. fluorescent
33. nominate

34. chair
35. length
36. advisable
37. beginning
38. totaling
39. dropping
40. scissors
41. research
42. exhaust
43. alliance
44. gesture
45. yield
46. ineligible
47. license
48. desk
49. already
50. recede
51. personnel
52. labeled
53. separate
54. turnover
55. impel
56. obscure
57. capacity
58. calendar (date)
59. erroneous
60. embarrassed
61. ceremony
62. manageable
63. wholesale
64. replace
65. magnify
66. humorous

67. noticeable
68. principle (rule)
69. tariff
70. disagreeable
71. durable
72. precision
73. malicious
74. punctuate
75. limited
76. require
77. illogical
78. fulfill
79. principal (head)
80. its (possessive)
81. leniency
82. remain
83. relay
84. where
85. agreeable
86. identical
87. likelihood
88. guarantee
89. opportunity
90. superintendent
91. loose
92. left
93. notifying
94. practicable
95. attorneys
96. meantime
97. nickel
98. committee
99. negotiate

100. concede	133. nineteenth	166. knowledge
101. neutralize	134. succeed	167. prepaid
102. forfeit	135. concealed	168. naive
103. omitted	136. comparable	169. recurrence
104. installment	137. obtainable	170. issuing
105. seize	138. bookkeeper	171. surprise
106. irreparable	139. remind	172. incredible
107. questionnaire	140. impatient	173. testimonial
108. familiar	141. occurrence	174. opponent
109. supersede	142. inferred	175. wagered
110. pessimistic	143. almanac	176. illegible
111. valuable	144. occasion	177. advocate
112. insistent	145. gauge	178. impossible
113. ninth	146. underwrite	179. voluntary
114. warehouse	147. grasp	180. interpretation
115. remittance	148. company	181. summarize
116. ambiguous	149. sympathy	182. hindrance
117. letterhead	150. lose	183. technical
118. salary	151. unduly	184. interfered
119. obstruct	152. imperative	185. unnecessary
120. justified	153. diligent	186. generalize
121. until	154. messenger	187. whether (if)
122. franchise	155. usable	188. indebtedness
123. realize	156. objectionable	189. beneath
124. peculiar	157. analysis	190. indefensible
125. exceed	158. recommend	191. triplicate
126. prescription	159. exercise	192. contribute
127. fragile	160. mediocre	193. obstinate
128. diplomatic	161. genuine	194. confirm
129. essential	162. mailman	195. travel
130. infinite	163. equipped	196. mileage
131. machinery	164. insignificant	197. assistance
132. arguing	165. enforceable	198. minimum

199. apologies	232. pamphlet	265. excellent
200. meanwhile	233. dilemma	266. amendment
201. sponsor	234. communicate	267. expression
202. moreover	235. package	268. counsel (advise)
203. appointment	236. effort	269. efficiency
204. merchandise	237. exhibitor	270. immediately
205. athletics	238. preliminary	271. disbursement
206. aluminum	239. repair	272. difficulty
207. electric	240. possession	273. literature
208. maintenance	241. employee	274. benefited
209. continuous	242. responsible	275. miscellaneous
210. mechanical	243. eligible	276. concur
211. contain	244. incidentally	277. necessarily
212. mortgage	245. balance	278. available
213. cooperate	246. claim	279. leisure
214. literally	247. vocabulary	280. criticize
215. consistent	248. colleague	281. oneself
216. movable	249. vehicle	282. deteriorate
217. authorize	250. grateful	283. accumulate
218. aspirant	251. verify	284. devastate
219. consensus	252. grievance	285. marriage
220. negative	253. commodity	286. office
221. annual	254. mailable	287. specialize
222. procedure	255. sacrifice	288. organize
223. dissatisfied	256. contrive	289. controlled
224. remove	257. transferring	290. dependent
225. economical	258. desolate	291. statistical
226. receive	259. excusable	292. envelope
227. expenditure	260. conferred	293. formerly
228. prejudice	261. parallel	294. liaison
229. disappoint	262. preference	295. secretary
230. relieve	263. notable	296. dialect
231. equally	264. earlier	297. schedule

298. diminish	331. enlightenment	364. retainer
299. encouragement	332. futurity	365. casualty
300. same	333. municipal	366. automatic
301. disappearance	334. modify	367. visualize
302. scarcely	335. discipline	368. should
303. pastime	336. remorse	369. evidence
304. eccentric	337. extremely	370. equity
305. favorable	338. default	371. counterfeit
306. referring	339. reimburse	372. accommodate
307. emphasis	340. revoke	373. reparation
308. privilege	341. multiply	374. inherent
309. fourth	342. financial	375. nuisance
310. similar	343. accustomed	376. tragedy
311. hesitate	344. executive	377. corridor
312. universal	345. congenial	378. fortunate
313. handsome	346. loneliness	379. innocence
314. owing	347. dictionary	380. auditor
315. development	348. merge	381. forgetting
316. compelled	349. record	382. achievement
317. uneasy	350. especially	383. exempt
318. program	351. penalize	384. ownership
319. percentage	352. memorandum	385. attention
320. desirable	353. commission	386. indicative
321. distributor	354. environment	387. confidential
322. eliminate	355. mutually	388. inspection
323. equilibrium	356. gratis	389. legacy
324. lying	357. logical	390. repetition
325. nevertheless	358. twentieth	391. luxury
326. essence	359. tracer	392. emergency
327. allowance	360. unfortunately	393. vacation
328. adjustable	361. deficient	394. remarkable
329. questionable	362. imitation	395. reasonable
330. collect	363. coordinate	396. spacious

397. connect
398. conduct
399. nonchalant
400. reinstate
401. siege
402 despair
403. forcibly
404. optimism
405. accountant
406. manual
407. announcement
408. profitable
409. approach
410. actually
411. serviceable
412. defendant
413. pursuing
414. sufficiency
415. provision
416. bulletin
417. exceptional
418. prestige
419. remembrance
420. abundance
421. official
422. arrears
423. unanimous
424. difference
425. censure
426. depository
427. division
428. victorious
429. fiscal

430. destination
431. considerably
432. amount
433. superior
434. pedestrian
435. experience
436. traditional
437. honorable
438. periodical
439. illiterate
440. government
441. legislate
442. penetrate
443. readily
444. proposal
445. insertion
446. perpetrate
447. regulation
448. specimen
449. performance
450. hazard
451. quotation
452. suggestion
453. distinction
454. studying
455. plan
456. congratulate
457. influence
458. portrait
459. substitute
460. frequency
461. misspell
462. integrity

463. unite
464. appropriate
465. currency
466. presentation
467. misfortune
468. strengthen
469. apparently
470. honorary
471. insurable
472. promissory
473. compensate
474. article
475. vacuum
476. warrant
477. diagram
478. recitation
479. beneficiary
480. compromise
481. recuperate
482. acceptance
483. utilize
484. acknowledge
485. constitute
486. number
487. catastrophe
488. liability
489. determination
490. intentionally
491. statute
492. absolutely
493. late
494. competent
495. admittance

496. recreation	529. serenity	562. probability
497. restitution	530. skeptical	563. demonstration
498. violence	531. perseverance	564. impediment
499. scarcity	532. equivalent	565. opinion
500. petition	533. applicable	566. endowment
501. filing	534. typewriter	567. controversy
502. tangible	535. lien	568. resume
503. prepare	536. assume	569. guidance
504. diseases	537. temporary	570. departure
505. ignorant	538. budgeting	571. inconvenience
506. scandal	539. inevitably	572. variety
507. significance	540. maximum	573. renewal
508. circumstances	541. auditorium	574. acquaintance
509. reliable	542. tax	575. texture
510. agencies	543. return	576. minority
511. eventually	544. persuade	577. patience
512. initial	545. immovable	578. security
513. addition	546. reduction	579. observance
514. interrupt	547. spontaneous	580. personality
515. ordinarily	548. scholastic	581. amateur
516. dominant	549. unconditional	582. estimate
517. conviction	550. handling	583. changeable
518. reservation	551. subtraction	584. tolerant
519. pronunciation	552. wrong	585. examination
520. appraisal	553. structural	586. incentive
521. correct	554. receipt	587. simplicity
522. disposition	555. engagement	588. collision
523. injustice	556. discuss	589. trivial
524. submission	557. disability	590. incurred
525. amusement	558. unprofitable	591. headache
526. improbable	559. ridiculous	592. carton
527. reputation	560. ruler	593. competition
528. opposite	561. tentative	594. reconciliation

595. abbreviate
596. illustration
597. commerce
598. inadequate
599. suspicious
600. dismissal

CHAPTER

23

Demons and Super-Demons

If you have studied the previous chapters, you are now probably an above-average speller. You spell better than 75 out of 100 randomly chosen persons.

Do you want to spell even better—to rank among the top ten per cent?

To reach that exalted level, you must master some well-known spelling demons, words with which even superior spellers like yourself have trouble.

The demons listed below will test your ability. They are difficult and confusing but can be mastered with a little study.

Admittedly some are rare, but not unusually so. They turn up in the reading and conversation of cultured people.

To help you master them, two kinds of help are given. First, infrequently used words are defined so that you will not have to run to a dictionary to discover their meaning. Secondly, the spelling difficulty in each word is italicized.

The exercises at the end of the chapter will test your spelling prowess. Don't undertake the exercises, however, without preliminary study. If you score a hundred in any exercise, you are one in ten thousand!

DEMONS! DEMONS! DEMONS!

abb*eys*

a*berr*ation

al*lelv*ia

ap*iary* (A place where bees are kept)

ap*pell*ation

a*que*ous

ar*c*tic

a*v*er

baci*llus*

bassin*et*

bes*tial*

bib*u*lous (Inclined to drink)

b*oui*llon

cad*uceu*s (The insignia of the Medical Corps, U.S. Army)

c*ait*iff (A mean and wicked person)

calor*ie*

cal*yx*

came*os*

cance*ll*ation

cant*icle* (A little song or hymn)

canva*ss* (The act of soliciting votes)

cara*fe* (A glass water bottle for the table)

cata*rrh*

c*au*l (A membrane which sometimes covers the head of a child at birth)

cell*ar*

cell*ular*

cet*ace*an (A whale)

ch*ai*se

chan*cre* (A venereal sore)

chatt*el* (Capital; principal)

cheru*bic*

chi*ffo*nier (A high and narrow chest of drawers)

chr*ysa*lis (The cocoon in which butterflies develop)

clay*ey*

client*ele*

cole slaw

coli*c*ky

co*lo*ssal

con*dign* (Fit, suitable; for example, condign punishment)

complaisance (Disposition to please)

con*n*oisseur

contract*i*ble

coo*lly*

corn*u*copia

coro*ll*ary

co*rr*oborate

coun*c*ilor (An advisor)

coun*sell*or (A lawyer)

covey
coxswain
crevasse (A deep crevice)
crewel (Worsted yarn, slackly
    twisted)
curacy (The office of a curate)
cynosure (A center of attrac-
    tion)
deign
dieresis (Two dots placed over
    a vowel to show that it is
    pronounced as a separate
    syllable)
diphtheria
distensible
donkeys
dowry
dyne (a unit of force)
dyspeptic
ebullient
empyrean (The heavens)
ephemeral (Lasting only a day)
Eskimos
excel
exegesis (A critical explana-
    tion of a text)
expansible
expiable (Capable of being
    atoned)
fezzes (Felt Turkish hats)
fieriest (Most fiery)
flexion (A movement of a
    joint)

fulsome
garlicky
garrote (To strangle)
genealogy
gneiss (A kind of rock)
gringos (As used contemptu-
    ously by Spanish-speaking
    people, Americans)
harakiri (Suicide by disem-
    bowelment)
hemorrhage
hoeing
imperceptible
infusible
isthmus
jinrikisha (A small two-
    wheeled vehicle drawn by
    a man)
khaki
kilos
kimono
labeled
larynx
lightning
lingoes
majordomos
mellifluous (Sweetened with
    honey)
mnemonics (The art of im-
    proving the memory)
penicillin
picnicking
perfectible

phleg*m*

queue

refer*r*er

*rh*eum (A watery discharge from the eyes or nose)

sacri*l*egious

sar*s*aparilla

*sc*imitar (A curved sword)

shellac*k*ed

sibilan*c*y

sing*e*ing

strait jacket

tread*le*

troll*eys*

vendi*b*le (Salable)

wir*y*

wr*ie*st (Most wry)

zw*ei*back

STUMP YOUR FRIENDS!

At your next party challenge the spelling ability of your friends. Distribute slips of paper and pencils, and dictate the following ten words. Scarcely anyone knows the spelling of all ten, as you will see.

A score of 7 is commendable; 8 is exceptional; 9 is incredible; and 10 is out of this world.

altos

colicky

ecstasy

hypocrisy

inoculate

liquefy

plague

rarify

supersede

vilify

Achievement Tests

NAME. . . . . .SCORE. . . . .

ACHIEVEMENT TEST 1
Chapters 1-4

Indicate by writing T or F to the right whether the following state-ments about English spelling are true or false.

1. English spelling is difficult because it is not phonetic.   . . . .
2. At one time in the history of English the endings in *through, thorough, plough* were pronounced.   . . . .
3. The element *pt* in *ptomaine, pterodactyl,* and *ptarmigan* is pronounced in Modern English.   . . . .
4. *Spaghetti, toreador, echelon,* and *sputnik* are derived from Italian, Spanish, French, and Russian respectively.   . . . .
5. Such words as *birth—berth, air—heir* are called antonyms.   . . . .
6. Many poor spellers do not hear words correctly.   . . . .
7. Nervous tension never interferes with inability to spell.   . . . .
8. There are no rules in spelling that are worth learning.   . . . .
9. The most reliable source of information for spelling is in the dictionary.   . . . .
10. Occasionally there are differences between British and American spelling.   . . . .

11. The sounds of English vowels have not changed through the centuries. · · · ·

12. The *K* in *knowledge,* and the *K* in *knee* were at one time pronounced in English. · · · ·

13. Good examples of homonyms are *fright—freight; sleigh—sleight; tray—trait.* · · · ·

14. Spelling *antidote* as *anecdote* may indicate poor or careless listening. · · · ·

15. Dictionaries vary their spelling in accordance with the areas of the country. · · · ·

16. To become a better speller you must read everything very slowly. · · · ·

17. Many good spellers can tell that a word is misspelled by its appearance (or configuration). · · · ·

18. All good spellers inherit this ability. · · · ·

19. Sometimes you can discover your own spelling devices to help you. · · · ·

20. A good way to recall the spelling of *stationary* is to think of *station.* · · · ·

21. The British prefer to add an extra *U* in such words as *labour, favour,* and *armour.* · · · ·

22. The section on correct spelling in a good dictionary is entitled *Orthography.* · · · ·

23. The words *center* and *centre* are examples of *homonyms.* · · · ·

24. The words *theater* and *theatre* are examples of *antonyms.* · · · ·

25. There is little value in compiling your own list of misspelled words. · · · ·

26. In learning how to spell the word *superintendent* it is advisable to pronounce each syllable distinctly. · · · ·

27. The letter *b* in *debt* and *doubt* is not pronounced in Modern English. · · · ·

28. In learning how to spell a new word it is helpful to write it several times correctly. . . . .

29. The trouble with English spelling is that there are no rules. . . . .

30. The ancient Sumerians used a language that was called hieroglyphics. . . . .

31. There is no difference in pronunciation between *trough* and *through*. . . . .

32. *Tough* and *rough* are homonyms. . . . .

33. *Through* and *true* have the same final sound. . . . .

34. The final sound in *knight* and *tight* is pronounced *īt*. . . . .

35. Many English words derived from ancient Greek have silent letters as in *psyllium* and *pseudonym*. . . . .

36. *Moat* and *mote* are examples of homonyms. . . . .

37. Words like *privilege* and *government* are frequently misspelled by omitting a letter. . . . .

38. Skimming will make one a better speller. . . . .

39. Careful observation helps one to become a better speller. . . . .

40. It is possible to train your eyes so they can recognize misspelled words by their appearance. . . . .

41. You can fix the correct spelling of the word *principle* by associating it with ru*le*. . . . .

42. To fix the correct spelling of *separate*, think of *sepa* plus *rate*. . . . .

43. By recalling the spelling of *where*, you may spell *there* correctly. . . . .

44. The words *hair* and *heir* are pronounced the same. . . . .

45. Though "practice makes perfect" many professional writers are sometimes plagued by misspellings. . . . .

46. The ultimate aim of learning to spell is to avoid consulting the dictionary. . . . .

47. If you read a printed article containing the words

savour and *connexion* you might conclude that the article was printed in England. . . . .

48. Some people might learn to spell *their* correctly by associating it with *heir*. . . . .

49. The words *rough* and *ruff* are true homonyms. . . . .

50. The words *sough* and *rough* are identical in sound. . . .

51. Words in English derived from ancient Greek are pronounced exactly as they were in Greece. . . . .

52. English words are spelled exactly as they sound. . . . .

53. The best way to study spelling is memorize all the words you need. . . . .

54. *Beet* and *beat* are true antonyms. . . . .

55. Because there are *gh* in *night* and *sight,* they should be pronounced. . . . .

56. A person writing *litature* instead of *literature* has probably not heard the word correctly. . . . .

57. Because the *b* in *debt* is silent, therefore the *b* in *debit* should also be silent. . . . .

58. An error in spelling *magazine* and *temperament* is that the middle *a* is frequently omitted. . . . .

59. To pronounce *scrambled* as *skwambled* may be due to infantile speech. . . . .

ACHIEVEMENT TEST 2.
Chapters 5-6

Underscore the word spelled correctly in the parentheses.

1. He wanted to buy a (low-priced, low priced) car.
2. This author was (best known, best-known) for his characterization.
3. She was the (thirty-first, thirty first) queen to be chosen.
4. This hypothesis was a little (far-fetched, far fetched).
5. The ewe was (newly-born, newly born).
6. It was the (highest priced, highest-priced) dress in the store
7. It was a successful (pre-election, preelection) bet.
8. To get this loan, you must have a (coowner, co-owner).
9. They cheered the (exGovernor, ex-Governor).
10. (Vice-Admiral, Vice Admiral) Rooney was promoted.
11. The doctors (conferred, confered) for two hours.
12. We had no (preference, preferrence) in this matter.
13. After many trials, he was (transferred, transfered) to another prison.
14. The girl quickly tore the (wrapings, wrappings) from the package.
15. Many new bills are thrown into the legislative (hoper, hopper).
16. Mulvaney was the best (hitter, hiter) in the league.
17. Turkey, plus all the (trimings, trimmings) was served yesterday.
18. The Dupont Company had a (controlling, controling) interest in the firm.
19. Our graduates (excelled, exceled) all others in Yale.
20. The prisoner never (regretted, regreted) his misdeeds.
21. The house had a (low-ceiling, low ceiling).

22. (One half, one-half) of the audience left at the end of the first act.
23. All night the tune kept (dining, dinning) in her head.
24. The duchess wore a (low necked, low-necked) gown at the party.
25. The employer demanded several (references, referrences).
26. We are all (hoping, hopping) for permanent peace.
27. Such freak accidents (occured, occurred) seldom.
28. The guilty culprit wore a (hangdog, hang-dog) look.
29. America at that time had (unparalleled, unparaleled) prosperity.
30. It was the (twenty ninth, twenty-ninth) celebration of the ending of the war.
31. The (pre-dawn, predawn) flight was a success.
32. My cousin was the (high scorer, high-scorer) in the game.
33. My mother always (prefered, preferred) to save rather than spend everything.
34. The (ex policeman, ex-policeman) was found guilty of perjury.
35. The judge and the attorneys (conferred, confered) for three hours.
36. The athlete (chined, chinned) thirty times on the horizontal bar.
37. The (Pro-Temperance, Pro Temperance) Party won few votes.
38. The poor little bird (flaped, flapped) her wings feebly and then remained still.
39. The (red-cheeked, red cheeked) youngster seemed shy.
40. Some of the guests at the home were over (eighty eight, eighty-eight) years old.
41. Television has been accused of (sub-liminal, subliminal) advertising.
42. The soldier seemed (regretful, regrettful) at his actions.
43. This rouge seems to be the (lowest priced, lowest-priced) in the entire shop.

44. Adolescents are frequently (smitten, smiten) with puppy love.
45. His appearance at the trial was (well-timed, well timed).
46. He was (hiting, hitting) well in that game.
47. The boy kept (running, runing) despite the cries of his mother.
48. Many guards (patroled, patrolled) the prison on the day of the execution.
49. Passengers should be (already, all ready) at 10 P.M.
50. A (run-on, run on) sentence contains more than enough for one complete sentence.
51. We greeted the (Senator-elect, Senator elect).
52. Rescue boats went back and forth in the (mid Atlantic, mid-Atlantic) area.
53. Her praises were (extoled, extolled) for her amazing performance.
54. Eisenhower's (aide-de-camp, aidedecamp) was later decorated for his contributions.
55. After a little encouragement the guitarist (regaled, regalled) the picnickers with many songs.
56. Mary won first prize; but Susan was (runner up, runner-up).
57. Mills for (spining, spinning) cotton have long supported the town.
58. A few parts of the story were (omitted, omited) by the defendant.
59. Children frequently (scraped, scrapped) their elbows at the corner.
60. Periods of prosperity have (recurred, recured) with regularity in this state.
61. Their marriage was (annuled, annulled) by mutual consent.
62. The nurse (scrubed, scrubbed) the baby's face until it was gleaming.
63. The crowd (paniced, panicked) after the accident.
64. South America (rebeled, rebelled) against the mother country.
65. Judge Harmon (deferred, defered) sentence until Friday.

ACHIEVEMENT TEST 3
Chapters 7-9

Underscore the word spelled correctly in the parentheses.

1. The agent signed the (receipt, reciept) for the rent.
2. It was a great (relief, releif) to go home at last.
3. Mary gave a loud (shriek, shreik) and ran.
4. The marines refused to (yeild, yield) their positions.
5. He was a perfect (fiend, feind) in his behavior.
6. His (acheivement, achievement) was remarkable.
7. Once we have lost our reputation, it is difficult to (retreive, retrieve) it.
8. It takes a good (freind, friend) to make one.
9. The slain leader was carried to the (beir, bier).
10. He was (chief, cheif) of the whole island.
11. We were (receiveing, receiving) visitors all day.
12. My father reminded us that we would be (dineing, dining) at six.
13. It was the loveliest sight (imagineable, imaginable).
14. (Judging, judgeing) from the attendance, the play was a hit.
15. Her success in college was (surpriseing, surprising).
16. Thoreau was (writeing, writing) a great deal while staying at Walden Pond.
17. The wounded dog was (whining, whineing) all night long.
18. All those (desireous, desirous) of success must work hard.
19. The (density, denscity) of the atmosphere is being studied.
20. The lecturer spoke clearly and (sincerely, sincerly).
21. Hailstones fell down several (chimneys, chimnies).
22. In this machine there were many levers and (pulleys, pullies)

23. The soldiers shot several (volleys, vollies) at their fleeing enemies.
24. The (salaries, salarys) of his employees were frequently raised.
25. The Greeks composed the greatest dramatic (tragedeys, tragedies).
26. The judge pronounced his sentence (angrily, angryly).
27. It is advisable occasionally to be (mercyful, merciful).
28. The band-leader played several (medleys, medlies).
29. A public (conveyance, conveyence) was supplied to the general.
30. Good carriage always (dignifies, dignifys) the person.
31. It is difficult to (deceive, decieve) people all the time.
32. Certain traits sometimes run in (families, familys).
33. We both like (dining, dineing) out frequently.
34. Strenuous efforts are required to (achieve, acheive) a scholarship.
35. This trail is not for the birds but for (donkeys, donkies).
36. Much (encouragment, encouragement) was required before the baby would walk.
37. Aeschylus wrote some of the greatest (tragedeys, tragedies) of all times.
38. Astronomers can now (percieve, perceive) stars that are quite small.
39. Space travel is no longer (unimagineable, unimaginable).
40. This line had the fewest (casualties, casualtys).
41. "Be (mercyful, merciful)," exclaimed the old lady.
42. We noticed that all the ants seemed (busily, busyly) engaged in building a new home.
43. Jascha Heifetz was (accompanied, accompanyed) by an accomplished pianist.
44. When her son did not return the mother was (worried, worryed).
45. After five (volleys, vollies), the soldiers put their guns aside.

46. Reynolds frequently (portrayed, portraied) the English nobility of the 18th Century.
47. His sermons frequently seemed touched with (sublimity, sublimeity).
48. Such actions at this time seemed (inadvisable, inadviseable).
49. By careless handling, she seemed to be (singing, singeing) her hair.
50. In expository writing (vagueness, vaguness) is not tolerated.
51. "Stop (argueing, arguing) and come away," the wife shouted to her husband.
52. Considering everything, it was a (lovely, lovly) wedding.
53. Such (couragous, courageous) action was rarely seen.
54. Dinner at this late hour was (tastless, tasteless).
55. Working long on the (contriveance, contrivance) made him a bit fanatic about it.
56. Our (neighbors, nieghbors) to the south were angry at our behavior.
57. Careless training may lead to such (mischievious, mischievous) behavior in childhood.
58. The last (frontier, fronteir) is now in space.
59. Although the (ceiling, cieling) was low, he bought the house.
60. Women are (desireous, desirous) of consideration from men.
61. The castle was (beseiged, besieged) for ten days.
62. Mary's (likeness, likness) was obvious in the portrait.
63. After many lessons he learned to dance (gracfully, gracefully).
64. This celebration was (truly, truely) magnificent.
65. The comic made his living by (mimicing, mimicking) others.

ACHIEVEMENT TEST 4
Chapters 10-12

Underscore the word spelled correctly in the parentheses.

1. All the (buffaloes, buffalos) were killed in this territory.
2. The President sent through his two (vetoes, vetos) to Congress.
3. All the (tomatoes, tomatos) had ripened.
4. We examined six (pianos, pianoes) before we selected one.
5. Cowboys learn how to do many stunts with their (lassoes, lassos).
6. Among the (calfs, calves) were some spotted ones.
7. All the (leafs, leaves) fell down.
8. Many old (beliefs, believes) must be disregarded.
9. Napoleon crushed many (armies, armys) in his time.
10. This farm still made use of (oxes, oxen).
11. Many college freshmen (don't, dont) know how to study.
12. This salesman specialized in (mens', men's) hosiery.
13. It was (his, his') greatest victory.
14. (Who'se, who's) there?
15. Dot all the (i's, is) and cross the (ts, t's).
16. "(Youve, you've) won your battle," said the trainer.
17. The shopper specialized in (lady's, ladies') shoes.
18. This was my (brother-in-law's, brother's-in-law's) house.
19. It was the (children's, childrens') ward to which we hurried.
20. This (couldn't, could'nt) have happened to a nicer chap.
21. It was once more a conflict between (East, east) and (West, west).
22. The young artists admired the works of (grandma Moses, Grandma Moses).

23. At the Sorbonne, he specialized in the (hindu, Hindu) languages.
24. My uncle belonged to the (elks, Elks).
25. The hit of the week was ("For my Beloved," "For My Beloved").
26. A popular novel in high school is (*A Tale of two Cities, A Tale of Two Cities*).
27. They traveled (North, north) for twenty miles.
28. On (Columbus Day, Columbus day), many stores are closed.
29. One of the greatest musical hits is (*My fair Lady, My Fair Lady*).
30. He was recently elected to the (house of representatives, House of Representatives).
31. The printer corrected the (proofs, prooves) of the new book.
32. After rounding up the young (calfs, calves), the cowboy rode back to the ranch.
33. My friend liked all his (brothers-in-law, brother-in-laws).
34. Count all the (7's, 7s) in this line!
35. Some ranches have as many as 10,000 (sheeps, sheep).
36. All the (alumni, alumnuses) of Fairweather College returned on Founder's Day.
37. Before the American public high schools, there were many (academies, academys).
38. It is very difficult to discover a single (curricula, curriculum) which can satisfy all people.
39. Ehrlich stained many (bacilli, bacilluses) in his career.
40. The (boy's, boys') hat was on crooked.
41. ("They're, theyr'e) here," the Captain shouted.
42. The conference passed a resolution against all high (doctor's, doctors') fees.
43. The numerous (teacher's, teachers') contributions were finally rewarded.

44. We enjoyed (Harrigan and Hart's, Harrigan's and Hart's) humor.
45. The sale took place in the (women's, womens') hosiery department.
46. "I never want to touch a penny of (their's, theirs)," she shouted.
47. All the (ts, t's) in this word are left uncrossed.
48. He admired his (lawyer's, lawyers') integrity.
49. (Anniversaries, anniversarys) should be celebrated properly.
50. A pair of (oxes, oxen) is a rarity on a farm today.
51. Ripe (tomatos, tomatoes) were hurled at the performer.
52. The "Ivy League" colleges are situated mostly in the (east, East).
53. After studying (french, French) literature he began to appreciate Moliere.
54. Higher (Mathematics, mathematics) fascinated Einstein at an early age.
55. (Governor, governor) Rockefeller has attempted to balance the state budget.
56. Several (captains, Captains) won their promotions in this campaign.
57. The fiftieth state in the union is (hawaii, Hawaii).
58. Mrs. Morrow wrote *North to the (Orient, orient)*.
59. Soon there will be one hundred members of the U. S. (Senate, senate).
60. On (arbor day, Arbor Day) an interesting ceremony took place.
61. Of all the novels read in high school (*Silas Marner, Silas marner*) seems to be most popular.
62. Great praise has come recently to (admiral, Admiral) Rickover.
63. A famous radio personality years ago was (uncle Don, Uncle Don).
64. This store had good bargains in (boys', boy's) shoes.
65. There are many fine students from the (south, South) in the colleges today.

ACHIEVEMENT TEST 5
Chapters 13-14

In the following sentences the italic words are sometimes correctly spelled; sometimes misspelled. In the spaces to the right, place C if the spelling is correct. Write the correct spelling for all misspelled words.

1. Our lighter team was at a *dissadvantage*. ....
2. Park all *disabled* cars here. ....
3. Any *mistatement* of fact will be punished. ....
4. The old man could not *reccollect* anything that had happened. ....
5. The doctor *recommended* an aspirin. ....
6. This procedure was an *inovation*. ....
7. Let us *rennovate* your apartment. ....
8. Actions such as these are *unatural*. ....
9. This apartment had been *unoccupied* for a month. ....
10. Congress tried to *overide* the veto. ....
11. For misbehaving the sergeant was *dimoted*. ....
12. Sugar will easily *disolve* in water. ....
13. As a lawyer Clarence Darrow was *preminent*. ....
14. One should always have some *anteseptic* handy for unexpected cuts. ....
15. His behavior under fire was *degrading*. ....

Select the correct choice of the two in parentheses:

16. By crossing the state border they ran into difficulty with the (intra-state, interstate) commission. ....
17. Do not (interrupt, interupt) an older person. ....
18. At the end of his letter he added a (poscript, postscript). ....

19. Many (suburban, subburban) communities are growing. . . .
20. When the lights blew out we called the (superrintend-
    ent, superintendent).
21. Quite a few hotels here welcome (transient, transent)
    guests. . . . .
22. The judge ruled that this evidence was not (admissible,
    admissable). . . . .
23. Such arguments are (laughible, laughable). . . . .
24. It was (unthinkable, unthinkible) that he could lose the
    game. . . . .
25. For many years he was the most (eligible, eligable)
    bachelor in town. . . . .
26. England has always been (invincible, invincable) in a
    crisis. . . . .
27. (Legible, legable) handwriting is a delight for the
    reader. . . . .
28. Make yourself (comfortable, comfortible). . . . .
29. Many foods are (perishible, perishable) unless properly
    refrigerated. . . . .
30. Evidence of the disease was not yet (demonstrable,
    demonstrible). . . . .

In the following sentences the italic words are sometimes cor-
rectly spelled; sometimes misspelled. In the spaces to the right,
place C if the spelling is correct. Write the correct spelling for all
misspelled words.

31. The debater made a *mistake*. . . . .
32. I don't *reccolect* what happened. . . . .
33. *Professional* ball-players receive high salaries. . . . .
34. His sleight of hand was *unoticeable*. . . . .
35. That player is vastly *overated*. . . . .
36. Sometimes it is better if one doesn't know his *anti-*
    cedents. . . . .

37. Iodine is still a popular *antiseptic*. . . . .
38. Don't *interrupt* me," she exclaimed. . . . .
39. Lincoln was not very happy when several states *seseded* from the Union. . . . .
40. The doctor diagnosed the disease as a *preforated* ulcer. . . . .
41. We must look at things in their proper *prespective*. . . . .
42. Let us *proceed* with the business. . . . .
43. Many a *percocious* child can learn how to play chess well. . . . .
44. This water is hardly *drinkible*. . . . .
45. Some mountains are *inaccessable*. . . . .
46. The *combustible* materials were placed in fire-proof bins. . . . .
47. Many an *eligable* bachelor has been attracted by a pretty young girl. . . . .
48. There are some schools for *incorrigible* youngsters. . . . .
49. "Such language is *detestable*," said the teacher. . . . .
50. He was an old *acquaintence*. . . . .
51. The face of the *defendent* became pale as the verdict was read. . . . .
52. Sometimes little things turn out to have great *significence*. . . .
53. The mechanics overhauled the airplane motor in a *hanger*. . . . .
54. The *collar* of his shirt was frayed. . . . .
55. The businessman advertised in a local newspaper for an experienced *stenographer*. . . . .
56. Most department store customers prefer to use an *escalator* when they wish to ascend to another floor. . . . .
57. The *radiater* of the car started to boil over in the hot weather. . . . .

58. Readers who disagree with a newspaper's editorial position should write a letter to the *editor*.   . . . .
59. One of the duties of a *superviser* is to train employees.   . . . .
60. The *purchaser* is protected by a money-back guarantee.   . . . .

ACHIEVEMENT TEST 6
Chapter 15

Select the correctly spelled word from the two in parentheses:

1. Teachers frequently give good (advice, advise) to their students. . . . .
2. England and the U. S. have long been (alleys, allies). . . . .
3. There is nothing as beautiful as a happy bride walking down the (isle, aisle). . . . .
4. My parents said that they were (already, all ready). . . . .
5. Frequently one can have an optical (illusion, allusion) after eyestrain. . . . .
6. The judge refused to (altar, alter) his decision. . . . .
7. (Altogether, all together) there were twelve cents in his pocket. . . . .
8. The casket was (borne, born) on the shoulders of the pallbearers. . . . .
9. There were several (angles, angels) on this picture by Raphael. . . . .
10. We ordered an upper (berth, birth) on the train to Chicago. . . . .
11. Father was almost (besides, beside) himself with grief. . . . .
12. (Break, brake) the news gently. . . . .
13. The baby's (breath, breathe) came in short spasms. . . . .
14. The cowboy grasped the horse by the (bridal, bridle). . . . .
15. Ward leaders tried to (canvass, canvas) the district. . . . .
16. In Washington we visited the beautiful (Capital, Capitol). . . . .
17. The angry principal began to (censure, censor) the students for misbehavior. . . . .

18. He could chop several (cords, chords) of wood each day. . . . .

19. The salesmen showed me several suits of (clothes, cloths). . . . .

20. In college, my brother took the pre-medical (course, coarse). . . . .

21. Don't forget to (complement, compliment) him on his good grades. . . . .

22. The German (consul, council) telegraphed to his ambassador in Washington. . . . .

23. The cook removed the (corps, core) of the apple. . . . .

24. Scientists are often (incredulous, incredible) of new theories. . . . .

25. Many authors like to keep (diaries, dairies) when they are young. . . .

26. Justice Oliver Wendell Holmes frequently would (dissent, descent) from his colleagues. . . . .

27. After the meat course, we had a delicious (dessert, dissert). . . . .

28. Da Vinci invented a (devise, device) to hurl cannon-balls. . . . .

29. Hamilton and Burr fought a (duel, dual) in New Jersey. . . . .

30. This spot was (formally, formerly) a cemetery. . . . .

31. For several (instance, instants) he remained quiet. . . . .

32. Through an (ingenious, ingenuous) trick the prisoner escaped. . . . .

33. Actresses like to receive (complements, compliments) for their performances. . . . .

34. There were thirteen delicious (deserts, desserts) on the menu. . . . .

35. The Dutch (consul, counsel) in New York helped us to obtain a visa. . . . .

36. The new President was (formally, formerly) inaugurated. . . . .
37. Good food in the barracks will help produce good (moral, morale). . . . .
38. A graduate of Harvard was the (personal, personnel) manager of the store. . . . .
39. Avogadro's (principal, principle) led to many other important discoveries. . . . .
40. This company advertises a fine quality of (stationery, stationary). . . . .
41. Standing in line for a token is often a (waste, waist) of valuable time. . . . .
42. New inventions (supersede, supercede) old customs. . . . .
43. It was an (excedingly, exceedingly) hot day. . . . .
44. Nothing (succeeds, suceeds) like success. . . . .
45. The parade (proceded, proceeded) without further interruption. . . . .
46. The magician created an optical (allusion, illusion) for us. . . . .
47. The West will not (accede, acede) to these demands. . . . .
48. After the waters (receeded, receded), we returned to our home. . . . .
49. The (corps, corpse) was taken to the morgue. . . .
50. The baby liked (it's, its) finger. . . . .
51. "It's (later, latter) than you think," the preacher said. . . . .
52. Four black-robed monks (led, lead) the way yesterday. . . . .
53. After the battle, the general called his (council, counsel) together. . . . .
54. Several (lose, loose) shingles fell down. . . . .
55. Liquor is not permitted to (minors, miners). . . . .
56. A world at (peace, piece) is a world of security. . . . .
57. It was as (plane, plain) as the nose on his face. . . . .
58. After the hike, the boys were (quite, quiet) starved. . . . .

Answer Key

▶ **CHAPTER 5**
Exercise 1/*Page 22*

1. C	6. C	11. X	16. X
2. X	7. C	12. X	17. X
3. X	8. X	13. X	18. C
4. C	9. C	14. C	19. C
5. C	10. C	15. X	20. C

Exercise 2/*Page 28*

1. sister-in-law	8. C	15. trade-in
2. man-of-war	9. C	16. C
3. aide-de-camp	10. C	17. C
4. run-on	11. runner-up	18. built-in
5. downstairs	12. drive-in	19. C
6. anti-American	13. C	20. broken-down
7. C	14. C	

▶ **CHAPTER 6**
Exercise 1/*Page 33*

1. cramping	5. looking	8. resting
2. drumming	6. nodding	9. rigging
3. grinning	7. paining	10. scrubbing
4. hitting		

Exercise 2/*Page 34*

1. deferred	3. shopping	5. nineteen
2. reference	4. disapproval	6. hitting

7. singeing	12. tireless	17. movable
8. famous	13. truly	18. committed
9. controlling	14. swimmer	19. equipage
10. repellent	15. trimmer	20. excelling
11. desiring	16. occurrence	

Exercise 3/*Page 35*

1. adapt	adapting	adapted
2. cramp	cramping	cramped
3. design	designing	designed
4. conceal	concealing	concealed
5. congeal	congealing	congealed
6. blot	blotting	blotted
7. stop	stopping	stopped
8. crush	crushing	crushed
9. excel	excelling	excelled
10. defer	deferring	deferred
11. envelop	enveloping	enveloped
12. extol	extolling	extolled
13. flutter	fluttering	fluttered
14. happen	happening	happened
15. hum	humming	hummed
16. level	leveling	leveled
17. quarrel	quarreling	quarreled
18. rub	rubbing	rubbed
19. signal	signaling	signaled
20. retreat	retreating	retreated

Exercise 4/*Page 36*

1. witty	8. profiteer	15. deferment
2. spinner	9. meeting	16. rubber
3. blotter	10. dryer	17. developer
4. designer	11. inhabitable	18. goddess
5. quizzical	12. toiler	19. druggist
5. shutter	13. putter	20. trapper
7. slipper	14. development	

▶ CHAPTER 7

Exercise 1/*Page 39*

1. tourneys	5. surveyed	8. relayed
2. allayed	6. portraying	9. delays
3. volleyed	7. journeyed	10. parlayed
4. alleys		

Exercise 2/*Page 41*

1. C	5. C	8. C
2. C	6. C	9. C
3. C	7. C	10. icily
4. attorneys		

Exercise 3/*Page 42*

1. prettiness	7. pitied	13. hurrying
2. pettiness	8. tallying	14. copier
3. steadying	9. buyer	15. sloppiness
4. readied	10. dutiful	16. livelihood
5. bullies	11. readiness	17. dutiful
6. airiness	12. carried	

▶ **CHAPTER 8**

Exercise 1/*Page 44*

1. pleasantry	5. rocketry	8. personality
2. artistry	6. sophistry	9. dialectical
3. portraiture	7. nationality	10. practicality
4. clockwise		

Exercise 2/*Page 47*

1. revering	8. stated	15. relieving
2. lovely	9. feted	16. procrastinating
3. purchasable	10. fined	17. imagined
4. extremely	11. diving	18. besieged
5. pleasurable	12. shoved	19. receiving
6. largely	13. devising	
7. nudged	14. deceived	

Exercise 3/*Page 48–49*

1. benefit	benefiting	benefited
2. commit	committing	committed
3. lure	luring	lured
4. refer	referring	referred
5. pine	pining	pined
6. elevate	elevating	elevated
7. propel	propelling	propelled
8. fit	fitting	fitted
9. recur	recurring	recurred
10. remit	remitting	remitted
11. open	opening	opened

12. club	clubbing	clubbed
13. plunge	plunging	plunged
14. singe	singeing	singed
15. pursue	pursuing	pursued
16. scare	scaring	scared
17. throb	throbbing	throbbed
18. trot	trotting	trotted
19. use	using	used
20. whip	whipping	whipped

Exercise 4/*Page* 53

1. agreement
2. amusement
3. careful
4. canoeing
5. coming
6. disagreeable
7. engagement
8. excitement
9. immensity
10. likely
11. safety
12. senseless
13. shining
14. enlargement
15. enticing
16. perceived
17. escaping
18. discharged
19. relieving
20. contrivance

Exercise 5/*Page* 54

The answers to this exercise are contained in the sentences among the words italicized.

Exercise 6/*Page* 55

1. scarcely
2. vengeance
3. truly
4. tasty
5. noticeable
6. changeable
7. perspiring
8. retiring
9. awful
10. wisdom
11. assurance
12. insurance
13. outrageous
14. serviceable
15. courageous
16. gorgeous
17. pronounceable

▶ **CHAPTER 9**

Exercise 1/*Page* 58

No answers are needed for this exercise since the correct spellings are given.

Exercise 2/*Page* 58

1. aggrieve
2. brief
3. friend
4. grieve
5. frontier
6. mischief
7. shield
8. shriek
9. wield
10. foreign
11. relieve
12. leisure

13. handkerchief   16. perceive   19. conceive
14. receipt   17. grief   20. veil
15. seize   18. niece

Exercise 3/*Page 61*
The answers to this exercise are incorporated in the sentences.

▶ **CHAPTER 10**
Exercise 1/*Page 65*
1. reproofs   9. puffs   15. troughs
2. reprieves   10. muffs   16. stilettos or
3. sieves   11. sloughs   stilettoes
4. halos or haloes 12. bassos or bassi, 17. sheaves
5. gulfs   after Italian 18 radios
6. coifs   13. mambos   19. calves
7. albinos   14. surfs   20. sylphs
8. shelves

Exercise 2/*Page 66*
1. abbeys   5. chimneys   8. keys
2. alleys   6. donkeys   9. pulleys
3. attorneys   7. journeys   10. turkeys
4. buoys

Exercise 3/*Page 70*
1. t's   7. courts-martial   13. surreys
2. Marys   8. lieutenant colonels 14. inequities
3. anniversaries   9. bays   15. satellites
4. dromedaries   10. trays   16. functionaries
5. kerchiefs   11. flurries   17. avocados
6. 4's   12. sulkies   18. dynamos

Exercise 4/*Page 71*
1. groceries   7. pounds   13. altos or alti (Ital.)
2. things   8. pieces   14. alleys
3. tomatoes   9. chocolates   15. journeys
4. potatoes   10. purchases   16. keys
5. avocados   11. adventures   17. days
6. quarts   12. sopranos or 18. events
                  soprani (Ital.)

▶ **CHAPTER 11**

Exercise 1/*Page 75–76*

1. The young girl's hat
2. The men's votes
3. The ladies' styles
4. The cats' paws
5. The sailors' decorations
6. The professor's hat
7. The woman's shoe
8. The soprano's voice
9. The dog's tail
10. don't
11. haven't
12. couldn't
13. You're
14. can't
15. It's
16. Let's
17. wouldn't

▶ **CHAPTER 12**

Exercise 1/*Page 79-80*

1. Hotel Westover
2. Buick
3. Decoration Day
4. North Side High School
5. *Mutiny on the Bounty*
6. Old French
7. English, Bible
8. Uncle
9. Fifth Avenue
10. Washington coffee
11. Britain
12. Bard College
13. *The Taming of the Shrew,* Shakespeare
14. English, French
15. Aunt Emily, West

▶ **CHAPTER 13**

Exercise 1/*Page 85*

circumscribe—draw limits
transcribe—write a copy
subscribe—sign one's name
describe—represent by words
proscribe—denounce and condemn
prescribe—dictate directions

Exercise 2/*Page 86*

1. misstep
2. misunderstood
3. dissimilar
4. re-echo
5. substandard
6. supersonic
7. pre-Columbian
8. anti-imperialist
9. circumnavigates
10. postoperative

Exercise 3/*Page 87*

1. persecuted
2. proceed
3. precocious
4. perspective
5. prescribe
6. perforated
7. produce
8. persist
9. perpetual
10. propose

▶ **CHAPTER 14**

Exercise 1/*Page 90*
The answers are contained in the exercise.

Exercise 2/*Page 91*
The answers are contained in the exercise.

Exercise 3/*Page 95*
1. compliment
2. remembrance
3. consistent
4. superintendent
5. dependent
6. existence
7. descendant
8. acquaintance
9. grievance
10. permanent
11. magnicent
12. brilliance
13. complimentary or complementary, depending upon meaning
14. convenience
15. abundance
16. guidance
17. conscience
18. coincidence
19. apparent
20. consequential

Exercise 4/*Page 95*
1. accidentally
2. critically
3. elementally
4. equally
5. exceptionally
6. finally
7. generally
8. incidentally
9. intentionally
10. ironically
11. logically
12. mathematically
13. practically
14. professionally
15. really
16. typically
17. usually
18. verbally
19. globally

Exercise 5/*Page 100*
1. advantageous
2. courageous
3. dolorous
4. perilous
5. mountainous
6. beauteous
7. desirous
8. piteous
9. troublous
10. mischievous
11. plenteous
12. adventurous
13. bounteous
14. dangerous
15. grievous
16. humorous
17. outrageous
18. duteous
19. libelous
20. poisonous

Exercise 6/*Page 102*
1. beggar
2. receiver
3. conductor

4. passenger	7. operator	9. supervisor
5. governor	8. dollar	10. stenographer
6. laborer		

Exercise 7/Page 107

1. b	8. b	14. b	20. b
2. a	9. b	15. b	21. a
3. a	10. b	16. a	22. a
4. a	11. a	17. a	23. b
5. b	12. b	18. a	24. b
6. a	13. b	19. b	25. b
7. a			

▶ **CHAPTER 15**

Exercise 1/Page 111

1. alter	5. aisle	8. altogether
2. borne	6. already	9. all ready
3. brake	7. all right	10. capital
4. capital		

Exercise 2/Page 113

1. Council	5. It's	8. counsel
2. complement	6. dissent	9. formerly
3. course	7. led	10. dual
4. desert		

Exercise 3/Page 115

1. minor	5. waist	8. stationery
2. peace	6. their	9. whose
3. plane—plain	7. too	10. They're
4. principal		

Exercise 4/Page 118

1. clothes	5. beside	8. ingenuous
2. later	6. emigrants	9. ally
3. consul	7. formally	10. allusions
4. advice		

Exercise 5/Page 120

1. morale	5. than	8. moral
2. quite	6. formally	9. quite
3. personnel	7. lose	10. than
4. loose		

▶ **CHAPTER 16**
Exercise 1/*Page 122*
The answers to this exercise are found in the passage.

▶ **CHAPTER 17**
Exercise 1/*Page 129*
1. hundred
2. modern
3. perspiration
4. western
5. relevant
6. cavalry
7. children
8. jewelry
9. larynx
10. pattern

▶ **CHAPTER 18**
Exercise 1/*Page 132*
1. pharmacy
2. photograph
3. C
4. C
5. frequently
6. either
7. machine
8. triumphant
9. people
10. C
11. receive
12. paragraph
13. series
14. convene
15. fatigue

Exercise 2/*Page 133*
1. troop
2. brutal
3. suitable
4. rooster
5. through
6. acoustic
7. aloof
8. ruler
9. bouquet
10. goose

Exercise 3/*Page 134*
Example: The *two* boys took *too* long *to* get dressed.

Exercise 4/*Page 135*
1. accord
2. C
3. occur
4. C
5. apprehend
6. approximately
7. applaud
8. suffer
9. button
10. alliance
11. C
12. occupied
13. different
14. grammar
15. C
16. appear
17. sufficient
18. attention
19. C
20. C

Exercise 5/*Page 136*
1. allege
2. longevity
3. angel
4. jostle
5. jealousy
6. suggest
7. cordial
8. soldier
9. gist
10. jeer

Exercise 6/*Page 138*

1. k	6. d	11. n
2. p	7. g	12. p
3. t	8. t	13. h
4. p	9. g	14. p
5. t	10. t	15. t

Exercise 7/*Page 138*

1. although
2. thoroughfare—through
3. bought—cough
4. ought
5. tough
6. drought—throughout
7. slough
8. cough

Exercise 8/*Page 140*

1. fright	5. slight	8. freight
2. weight	6. tight	9. playwright
3. might	7. night	10. sight
4. neighbor		

Exercise 9/*Page 141*

1. spectacle	5. study	8. tradition
2. attention	6. pronunciation	9. stomach
3. statue	7. space	10. production
4. construction		

▶ CHAPTER 19

Exercise 1/*Page 146*

1. Sec. or Secy.	8. M.D.	15. Dept.
2. Treas.	9. Hon.	16. lb.
3. C.O.D.	10. yr.	17. Messrs.
4. A.M.	11. Sat.	18. D.D.S.
5. Jr.	12. R.F.D.	19. Rev.
6. doz.	13. R.S.V.P.	20. Blvd.
7. Aug.	14. Esq.	

Exercise 2/*Page 146*

1. Doctor of Philosophy
2. Avenue
3. inch
4. et cetera (and so forth)
5. number
6. Brothers
7. Postscript
8. Railroad
9. September
10. Freight on Board

11. Professor
12. Assistant
13. Eastern Standard Time
14. Governor
15. before Christ
16. anno Domini
17. Steamship
18. Street
19. received
20. department
21. Doctor of Medicine
22. Treasurer
23. Saturday
24. Honorable
25. Reverend
26. Secretary
27. Doctor of Dental Surgery
28. Captain
29. March
30. post meridiem (after noon)

▶ **CHAPTER 20**
Exercise 1/*Page 154*

1. a
2. c
3. a
4. d
5. d
6. b
7. b
8. b
9. c
10. a
11. b
12. d
13. c
14. d
15. a

▶ **CHAPTER 21**
Exercise 1/*Page 158*

1. C
2. C
3. definitive
4. C
5. C
6. C
7. undefinable
8. undesirable
9, pitiless
10. C
11. C
12. C
13. C
14. C
15. C
16. C
17. non-existent
18. preferable
19. C
20. unendurable
21. necessarily
22. C
23. C
24. changeable
25. judgment or judgement (Web. Collegiate)
26. accommodate
27. guarantee
28. receipts
29. C
30. C
31. chosen
32. possessed
33. recognized
34. sincerity
35. existence
36. embarrassed
37. C
38. excitable
39. preferred
40. occasion

▶ **ACHIEVEMENT TEST 1**
Chapters 1–4/*Page 177*

1. T
2. T
3. F
4. T
5. F
6. T
7. F
8. F
9. T
10. T
11. F
12. T

13. F	25. F	37. T	49. T
14. T	26. T	38. F	50. F
15. F	27. T	39. T	51. F
16. F	28. T	40. T	52. F
17. T	29. F	41. T	53. F
18. F	30. F	42. F	54. F
19. T	31. F	43. T	55. F
20. T	32. F	44. F	56. T
21. T	33. T	45. T	57. F
22. T	34. T	46. T	58. T
23. F	35. T	47. T	59. T
24. F	36. T	48. T	

▶ ACHIEVEMENT TEST 2
Chapters 5–6/*Page 181*

1. low-priced
2. best known
3. thirty-first
4. far fetched
5. newly born
6. highest priced
7. pre-election
8. co-owner
9. ex-Governor
10. Vice-Admiral
11. conferred
12. preference
13. transferred
14. wrappings
15. hopper
16. hitter
17. trimmings
18. controlling
19. excelled
20. regretted
21. low ceiling
22. one half
23. dinning
24. low-necked
25. references
26. hoping
27. occurred
28. hangdog
29. unparalleled
30. twenty-ninth
31. predawn
32. high scorer
33. preferred
34. ex-policeman
35. conferred
36. chinned
37. Pro-Temperance
38. flapped
39. red-cheeked
40. eighty-eight
41. subliminal
42. regretful
43. lowest priced
44. smitten
45. well timed
46. hitting
47. running
48. patrolled
49. all ready
50. run-on
51. Senator-elect
52. mid-Atlantic
53. extolled
54. aide-de-camp
55. regaled
56. runner-up
57. spinning
58. omitted
59. scraped
60. recurred
61. annulled
62. scrubbed
63. panicked
64. rebelled
65. deferred

▶ ACHIEVEMENT TEST 3
Chapters 7–9/*Page 185*

1. receipt
2. relief
3. shriek
4. yield
5. fiend
6. achievement
7. retrieve
8. friend
9. bier
10. chief
11. receiving
12. dining

13. imaginable
14. judging
15. surprising
16. writing
17. whining
18. desirous
19. density
20. sincerely
21. chimneys
22. pulleys
23. volleys
24. salaries
25. tragedies
26. angrily
27. merciful
28. medleys
29. conveyance
30. dignifies
31. deceive
32. families
33. dining
34. achieve
35. donkeys
36. encouragement
37. tragedies
38. perceive
39. unimaginable
40. casualties
41. merciful
42. busily
43. accompanied
44. worried
45. volleys
46. portrayed
47. sublimity
48. inadvisable
49. singeing
50. vagueness
51. arguing
52. lovely
53. courageous
54. tasteless
55. contrivance
56. neighbors
57. mischievous
58. frontier
59. ceiling
60. desirous
61. besieged
62. likeness
63. gracefully
64. truly
65. mimicking

▶ ACHIEVEMENT TEST 4
Chapters 10–12/*Page 189*

1. buffaloes, buffalos, buffalo
2. vetoes
3. tomatoes
4. pianos
5. lassos, lassoes
6. calves
7. leaves
8. beliefs
9. armies
10. oxen
11. don't
12. men's
13. his
14. who's
15. i's
16. you've
17. ladies'
18. brother-in-law's
19. children's
20. couldn't
21. East, West
22. Grandma Moses
23. Hindu
24. Elks
25. "For My Beloved"
26. *A Tale of Two Cities*
27. north
28. Columbus Day
29. My Fair Lady
30. House of Representatives
31. proofs
32. calves
33. brothers-in-law
34. 7's
35. sheep
36. alumni
37. academies
38. curriculum
39. bacilli
40. boy's
41. They're
42. doctors'
43. teachers'
44. Harrigan and Hart's
45. women's
46. theirs
47. t's
48. lawyer's
49. anniversaries
50. oxen
51. tomatoes
52. East
53. French
54. mathematics
55. Governor
56. captains
57. Hawaii
58. Orient
59. Senate
60. Arbor Day
61. *Silas Marner*
62. Admiral
63. Uncle Don
64. boys'
65. South

▶ **ACHIEVEMENT TEST 5**
Chapters 13–14/*Page 193*

1. disadvantage	21. transient	41. perspective
2. C	22. admissible	42. C
3. misstatement	23. laughable	43. precocious
4. recollect	24. unthinkable	44. drinkable
5. C	25. eligible	45. inaccessible
6. innovation	26. invincible	46. C
7. renovate	27. legible	47. eligible
8. unnatural	28. comfortable	48. C
9. C	29. perishable	49. C
10. override	30. demonstrable	50. acquaintance
11. demoted	31. C	51. defendant
12. dissolve	32. recollect	52. significance
13. pre-eminent	33. C	53. hangar
14. antiseptic	34. unnoticeable	54. C
15. C	35. overrated	55. C
16. interstate	36. antecedents	56. C
17. interrupt	37. C	57. radiator
18. postscript	38. C	58. C
19. suburban	39. seceded	59. supervisor
20. superintendent	40. perforated	60. C

▶ **ACHIEVEMENT TEST 6**
Chapter 15/*Page 197*

1. advice	21. compliment	40. stationery
2. allies	22. consul	41. waste
3. aisle	23. core	42. supersede
4. all ready	24. incredulous	43. exceedingly
5. illusion	25. diaries	44. succeeds
6. alter	26. dissent	45. proceeded
7. altogether	27. dessert	46. illusion
8. borne	28. device	47. accede
9. angels	29. duel	48. receded
10. berth	30. formerly	49. corpse
11. beside	31. instance	50. its
12. break	32. ingenious	51. later
13. breath	33. compliments	52. led
14. bridle	34. desserts	53. council
15. canvass	35. consul	54. loose
16. Capitol	36. formally	55. minors
17. censure	37. morale	56. peace
18. cords	38. personnel	57. plain
19. clothes	39. principle	58. quite
20. course		